CALIFORNIA'S DEADLY WOMEN

Murder and Mayhem in the Golden State

1850-1950

DEDICATION

Christyn, in the vastness of space and time, it has been one of my greatest joys to spend this lifetime with you. None of this would be possible without your support, and this book is lovingly dedicated to you.

CALIFORNIA'S DEADLY WOMEN

MURDER AND MAYHEM IN THE GOLDEN STATE

1850–1950

MICHAEL THOMAS BARRY

Schiffer Publishing Ltd

4880 Lower Valley Road • Atglen, PA 19310

Cover design by Brenda McCallum
Interior design by Matthew Goodman

Type set in Bad Neighborhood, Kings Typewriter 2, Bembo, Trade Gothic

ISBN: 978-0-7643-5530-1
Printed in China

Published by Schiffer Publishing, Ltd.
4880 Lower Valley Road
Atglen, PA 19310
Phone: (610) 593-1777; Fax: (610) 593-2002
E-mail: Info@schifferbooks.com
Web: www.schifferbooks.com

For our complete selection of fine books on this and related subjects, please visit our website at www.schifferbooks.com. You may also write for a free catalog.

Schiffer Publishing's titles are available at special discounts for bulk purchases for sales promotions or premiums. Special editions, including personalized covers, corporate imprints, and excerpts, can be created in large quantities for special needs. For more information, contact the publisher.

We are always looking for people to write books on new and related subjects. If you have an idea for a book, please contact us at proposals@schifferbooks.com.

CONTENTS

Prologue: The Female of the
Species by Rudyard Kipling . . . 12

Introduction . . . 15

CHAPTER ONE
Murder and Mayhem of the Victorian Age (1850–1899)

20	A Lynching in Downieville–Josefa Segovia (1851, Gold Country)
23	The Lady in Black–Laura Fair (1870, San Francisco)
27	A Virtuous Woman Turns to Murder–Lastenia Abarta (1881, Los Angeles)
30	The She-Devil–Hattie Woolsteen (1887, Los Angeles)
35	A Battered Woman–Isabella Andross (1887, San Pedro)
38	An Abusive Husband Gets His Just Rewards–Bridget Waters (1888, Los Angeles)
41	Tragedy in Tustin–Effie Scholl (1889, Orange County)
44	Never Take Candy from a Stranger–Cordelia Botkin (1898, San Francisco)

48   Brutal Bride—Katie Cook
(1899, Orange County)

CHAPTER TWO
Dastardly Deeds in the Early Decades of the Twentieth Century (1900–1919)

53   Old West Justice—Clara Wellman
(1901, Riverside County)

54   The Trunk Murderess—Emma LeDoux
(1906, Stockton)

58   Murder, He Wrote—Aurelia Scheck
(1906, Los Angeles)

60   The Red Murderess—Dora Chipp
(1906, Humboldt County)

62   Killing on Principle—Angela De Vita
(1910, Los Angeles)

63   A Woman's Desperation—Lea Delmon
(1913, Los Angeles)

65   The Money Maniac—Anna Hammond
(1917, Fresno County)

67   Murder or Suicide?—Gertrude Gibbons
(1918, Los Angeles)

CHAPTER THREE
Notorious Crimes of the
Roaring Twenties (1920–1929)

71 A Contemptuous Paramour's Ultimate Demise—Marie Leonard Bailey (1920, Pasadena)

73 The Black Widow—Louise Peete (1920–1947, Los Angeles)

79 A Matter of Life and Death—Nettie Platz (1921, Los Angeles County)

80 Love, Betrayal, and Tragedy—Madalynne Obenchain (1921, Los Angeles)

86 A Ghost in the Attic—Walburga "Dolly" Oesterreich (1922, Los Angeles)

90 The Tiger Woman—Clara Phillips (1923, Los Angeles)

94 Baby Borgia - Alsa Thompson (1925, Los Angeles)

96 A Mother's Pain—Edna May Fuller (1926, San Francisco)

98 Arsenic and Old Lace—Mary Hartman (1927–1930, Long Beach)

100 The Borgia of the Sierras—Eva Brandon Rablen (1929, Tuolumne County)

102 The Baby Blues—Josephine Valenti (1929, Los Angeles)

104 The Jimmy Valentine Burglary—Mary Kavanaugh (1929, Los Angeles)

CHAPTER FOUR
Infamous Criminalities of the
Great Depression (1930–1939)

107 Beware of the Black Hand—Rosa Tarlazzi (1930, East Los Angeles)

109 A Clear Case of Child Abuse—Custodia Vasquez Murillo (1930, East Los Angeles)

110 Poisoned for Profit—Anna Erickson and Esther Carlson (1931, Los Angeles County)

114 Spurned Affection—Nellie Burdick (1933, Berkeley)

116 The Enigma Woman—Nellie May Madison (1934, Los Angeles)

119 A Great Miscarriage of Justice—Bertha Talkington (1934, Merced County)

122 A Plea for Help—Edna Beatrice Mallette (1939, Los Angeles)

CHAPTER FIVE
Sensational Murders of the War Years
and Beyond (1940–1950)

126 An Unjust Sentence—Beatrice May Cox (1940, San Diego County)

128 Too Good to Live and Too Young to Die—Betty Hardaker (1940, Montebello)

131 A Bad Seed?—Chloe Davis (1940, Los Angeles)

134	The Duchess—Juanita Spinelli (1940, San Francisco & Sacramento)
138	Mary Anna Took an Axe and Gave Her Daughter Forty Whacks—Mary Anna Cox (1944, Placerville)
139	A Shakespearean Tragedy—Annie Irene Mansfeldt (1945, San Francisco)
144	Murder on the Yacht—Beulah Overell (1947, Newport Beach)
148	A Desire to Kill—Louise Gomes (1947, Sacramento County)
151	Pushing up Daisies—Ada Roberts Peters (1948, Tuolumne County)
153	Sex, Money, and Murder in Hancock Park—Betty Ferreri (1948, Los Angeles)

Conclusion . . . 157

Afterword: by Jill Leslie Rosenbaum, Ph.D., Professor of Criminal Justice . . . 159

Bibliography . . . 166

Index . . . 169

PROLOGUE

The Female of the Species

Rudyard Kipling

When the Himalayan peasant meets the he-bear in his pride,
He shouts to scare the monster, who will often turn aside.
But the she-bear thus accosted rends the peasant tooth and nail.
For the female of the species is more deadly than the male.

When Nag the basking cobra hears the careless foot of man,
He will sometimes wriggle sideways and avoid it if he can.
But his mate makes no such motion where she camps beside the trail.
For the female of the species is more deadly than the male.

When the early Jesuit fathers preached to Hurons and Choctaws,
They prayed to be delivered from the vengeance of the squaws.
'Twas the women, not the warriors, turned those stark enthusiasts pale.
For the female of the species is more deadly than the male.

Man's timid heart is bursting with the things he must not say,
For the Woman that God gave him isn't his to give away;
But when hunter meets with husband, each confirms the other's tale—
The female of the species is more deadly than the male.

Man, a bear in most relations—worm and savage otherwise—
Man propounds negotiations, Man accepts the compromise.
Very rarely will he squarely push the logic of a fact
To its ultimate conclusion in unmitigated act.

Fear, or foolishness, impels him, ere he lay the wicked low,
To concede some form of trial even to his fiercest foe.
Mirth obscene diverts his anger—Doubt and Pity oft perplex
Him in dealing with an issue—to the scandal of The Sex!

But the Woman that God gave him, every fibre of her frame
Proves her launched for one sole issue, armed and engined for the same;
And to serve that single issue, lest the generations fail,
The female of the species must be deadlier than the male.

She who faces Death by torture for each life beneath her breast
May not deal in doubt or pity—must not swerve for fact or jest.
These be purely male diversions—not in these her honour dwells.
She the Other Law we live by, is that Law and nothing else.

She can bring no more to living than the powers that make her great
As the Mother of the Infant and the Mistress of the Mate.
And when Babe and Man are lacking and she strides unclaimed to claim
Her right as femme (and baron), her equipment is the same.

She is wedded to convictions—in default of grosser ties;
Her contentions are her children, Heaven help him who denies!—
He will meet no suave discussion, but the instant, white-hot, wild,
Wakened female of the species warring as for spouse and child.

Unprovoked and awful charges—even so the she-bear fights,
Speech that drips, corrodes, and poisons—even so the cobra bites,
Scientific vivisection of one nerve till it is raw
And the victim writhes in anguish—like the Jesuit with the squaw!

So it comes that Man, the coward, when he gathers to confer
With his fellow-braves in council, dare not leave a place for her
Where, at war with Life and Conscience, he uplifts his erring hands
To some God of Abstract Justice—which no woman understands.

And Man knows it! Knows, moreover, that the Woman that God gave him
Must command but may not govern—shall enthrall but not enslave him.
And She knows, because She warns him, and Her instincts never fail,
That the Female of Her Species is more deadly than the Male.

-Rudyard Kipling's Verse: Inclusive Edition, 1885-1918.

"Women and elephants never
forget an injury."

-H. H. Munro (1870-1916)
Author and playwright

Introduction

There's an old saying in the news business: If it bleeds, it leads. The nightly news and other media outlets are filled with stories of crime, killing, and sorrow. But here's the dirty little secret: they wouldn't show us all that murder and mayhem if we didn't covertly crave it. Deep down, psychologically, we all want a glimpse of the darker side of humanity—but from the safety of our living rooms and recliners.

Within these pages are discussed some of the most notorious murders and shocking crimes ever committed by women in the state of California between 1850 and 1950. Some of the notorious cases discussed include candy poisoner Cordelia Botkin, trunk murderess Emma LeDoux, Black Widow serial killer Louise Peete, The Duchess Juanita Spinelli, and cleaver widow Betty Ferreri.

At one point the crimes of these women and others horrified the collective imagination of the state and nation, but for one reason or another many have faded away from our historical consciousness. The forty-six crime cases discussed in this book are presented in chronological order and are not an all-inclusive anthology of crime in California. The overall purpose is intended to be an introductory and brief examination of the cases discussed.

In choosing which crimes to include in this book, an eye was kept on the well-known and obvious, as well as more obscure stories. The objective is not to glorify criminals or the crimes they committed, rather it is deliberately written to be an unbiased description of facts. From this it is hoped that the reader will get a better understanding of the psychology and senselessness of these terrible acts. Some of the following accounts are more sensational than others, some more baffling, some more audacious, while almost all are shocking and appalling. The notorious crimes perpetrated by females revisited in this book are all of these things and much more.

When writing about crimes, especially those committed by women, many authors tend to embellish and exaggerate the wrongdoing as proof of the potential deadliness of the fairer sex. But in recent years the study of females and the crimes they commit have turned to a more feminist approach and have incorporated a movement toward socioeconomic reasons as to why women are driven to commit crime.

According to a US Department of Justice report on homicide statistics in the United States, one out of every ten murders are committed by women. Forensic psychologists have reported that females who kill often have backgrounds and motivations that differ greatly from their male counterparts. It was discovered that female murderers are more likely to be related to their victims, are less likely to plan their crime in advance, and are less likely to use extreme methods of violence. Traditionally, the role of women in society is to nurture, not to kill, but when this happens, it is most often committed in self-defense or reflective of some kind of mental illness.

The method of operation (*modus operandi*) of women killers often differs from men in how, why, and whom they kill. Historically, women have been characterized as accomplices or victims of male persuasion. While murder for men can involve many different motivations, the reports on women generally link their crimes with passion.

As a general rule, females tend to perpetrate "softer" forms of homicide, such as strangulation, suffocation, and poisoning. They are often more practical in their methods, using just enough violence to get the job done, and they are more driven by the end result, of someone being dead, than the actual act of killing itself. For women, the act of murder is often considered the last resort and seen as a defensive action, whereas for men it's almost always offensive in nature. Women often resort to murder after being sexually or emotionally abused. While generally they often share a common trait of suffering from some sort of physical or emotional trauma, they tend to commit these crimes as a pathological need for attention, control, or to simply express their anger.

Throughout history, lone female serial killers have been very rare and have often been part of a criminal couple; in such instances, murders are shared between the male and female partners or the woman has become infatuated with a more dominant male figure. In this case, women kill for much the same reasons as men: power, sexual hedonism, control, or financial gain. In terms of characteristics, both male and female serial killers often tend to be drifters who are disconnected from society; both have limited capacity for remorse and are often driven by an overriding psychological need to kill for the thrill of it.

It has been said in reference specifically to serial killers that murder is an act of transcendence, offering passage beyond social institutions in which the perpetrator feels trapped and affording the killer the power to act freely, unhampered by the structures of social life. It is possible that this can be extended toward murder in general. It is interesting to consider the low number of female murderers and the virtual nonexistence of female serial killers in the context of this definition. If murder offers power over oneself, why would women not take this opportunity to free themselves from the often-oppressive situations they find themselves in?

In a society that places importance on independence and individuality while at the same time restricting that individuality within societal boundaries, both males and females would have tensions within themselves. Under the right circumstances, these tensions would lead them to commit violent acts against those boundaries personified in other individuals. Some have taken the data of the majority of murders being committed by men as a sign that violence is a key part of a patriarchal society. The act of transcendence, murder, (if it is an act of transcendence) gives power only during the period the agent is not defined by society. Punishment is society's way of removing this power. Labeling a person as a criminal places them squarely outside of society and makes them subject to punishment. Their power is taken away by the controlling act of definition. The power comes from danger, and the person only poses a threat when they are still in society but uncontrolled by it.

Another theory on murder is that it is a desperate bid for empowerment in the face of the impossibility of perfection. In this sense, murder is committed when a person is faced with limitations. Certainly there is support for this in the data on infanticide. The mothers who were convicted were more likely to be young, single, and economically impoverished. The choice to dispose of an infant in this case seems related to the probable hardships the mother and her offspring would have faced in the future, making this an act of frustration over inability to transcend circumstances.

The taking of another person's life and the capacity to do so, gives the perpetrator a type of power. In the past, the percentage of female suspects convicted for murder has been less than the percentage of men. In medieval courts, women were acquitted more often than men for murder; this trend continued throughout the colonial period and into the early twentieth century in the United States. Between World War II and the Vietnam War, female suspects were convicted at a lower rate and for lesser degrees of homicide than males.

Historically, there has been a general leniency toward women who kill, and this comes from the traditional view of the male-dominated legal profession that viewed women as the weaker sex. For those with a worldview that insists women must be protected because they are weaker, it is easier to see these female criminals as being mentally unstable rather than to see them as capable of premeditation and intent. This view has resulted in fewer convictions and lesser sentences. We, as a society, are almost always more shocked by the acts of female killers, because women are commonly viewed as givers of life, and to take a life is seen as an aberration of nature. Although violent crimes, such as murder, committed by women are rare, they often hold the media and public spellbound.

It should be noted that by no means should all of the females discussed in this book necessarily be regarded as murderers. Some killed in self-defense and were acquitted, while others were found guilty and imprisoned or executed. Nonetheless, these are all accounts of females who were at one point accused of, or tried for, murder and other crimes. In the process of revisiting the crimes discussed in the following pages, it is hoped the reader will gain valuable insight into the facts, shifting perceptions, and values of the time period in which these deplorable acts were committed.

CHAPTER ONE

Murder and Mayhem of the Victorian Age

(1850-1899)

"Crime and punishment grow out of one stem. Punishment is a fruit that, unsuspected, ripens with the flower of the pleasure that concealed it."

–Ralph Waldo Emerson (1803-1882)
Poet, essayist, and lecturer.

A Lynching in Downieville
JOSEFA SEGOVIA
(1851, Gold Country)

The bold, impulsive, and rumbustious atmosphere in California during the Gold Rush era was apparent in the state's approach and swift punishment with regard to lawlessness. In the mining areas of northern California, fortune-seekers were so plentiful, and unruliness was such a problem that government agencies and law enforcement officials could not keep pace. The miners, therefore, had to remedy the situation with their own brand of justice that was swift and merciless to regulate their relationships with one another. Improvised courts were convened for the adjudication of disputes and for the trial of criminal suspects. The judgments and punishments of these hastily convened courts of law were immediate and severe. The miners' preference seemed to be for the simplest procedures possible. Their fundamental premise was that every citizen should be free to do as he or she pleased as long as he or she did not harm his or her neighbor. Violators of this code were dealt with swiftly and harshly so that they could not commit the offense again.

In detail, these proceedings varied from camp to camp, but in general, suspected thieves or murderers were hauled before these impromptu tribunals, testimony was heard, a jury returned a swift verdict, and the sentence was carried out immediately. Because imprisonment was not an option due to limited jail space, execution and banishment were the customary sentences. Some historians have suggested that miners' justice was no justice at all; with the innocent suffering as often as the guilty, there was only a haphazard correlation between crime and punishment. The following tale is a sad reminder of the failings and shortcomings of this style of frontier justice.

The 1851 Independence Day celebration in Downieville was a colorful and festive event that included political speeches and a grand parade down Main Street. Nearly 5,000 people, mostly local gold miners and camp hangers-on, crammed the streets of the tiny town. Most were in a cheerful mood, ready to drink and gamble in honor of America's seventy-fifth anniversary of the signing of the Declaration of Independence.

The Downieville of the early 1850s was little more than a dirt-filled road lined with saloons, gambling halls, and whorehouses. The town was situated at the convergence of the Downie and Yuba Rivers, and the hills surrounding the town were populated with hundreds of gold mines. Settled in late 1849, the town was first known as "The Forks" for its geographical location. It was renamed after William Downie, a Scotsman and military man who led an expedition up the North Fork of the Yuba River. He was also the town's first mayor. Downieville reached its peak population in 1851, with a population of 5,000 but steadily declined in the coming decades as gold became less plentiful.

But this celebration of our nation's birth was fated to be long remembered in Downieville not for its joyous celebration but for the awful events that were to unfold. These tragedies would forever leave a black mark on the history of the town and region. The frivolities and festivities lasted into the early morning hours of July 5, but several miners, including Fred Cannon and others, were in no mood to end the revelries. The men were drunk and ready to cause trouble. Cannon, who stood six-foot-four and weighed nearly 250 pounds, was an intimidating figure. Like so many of his contemporaries, he had arrived in the gold fields of California in search of fortune and fame, but he found little of both. Although he was an imposing hulk of a man, many of his friends described him as cheerful and easygoing when he wasn't drinking.

There are several different versions of the events that unfolded that night, and one popular but unsubstantiated account alleged that Cannon and his friends attempted to reignite the waning celebrations by banging on doors. One such home was the residence of a beautiful twenty-six-year-old Mexican woman named Josefa Segovia (also known as Juanita), a barmaid and common-law wife of a local gambler. There is much debate among historians about her life, and very little information has been uncovered. It is believed that she was originally from Sonora, Mexico, and was one of only a handful of women who lived in the area. Because of this, she and the other women were often targets of sexual harassment from miners who craved female companionship. Josefa was known to be quite feisty and had a very short temper. Fred Cannon was alleged to be one of her regular tormentors and harassers.

As Josefa was cleaning up and preparing for bed in the early morning hours of July 5, Cannon and his companions began pounding on the front door of her home. Their knocking was so hard that the door broke and came off its hinges. Josefa pleaded with the men to leave and angrily demanded they fix the damaged door. Cannon refused and exchanged insults with Josefa before reluctantly departing.

The next morning, a regretful Cannon allegedly told several associates that he was going to apologize for his rude behavior and went to Josefa's house. When he arrived at her home, she was in no mood to accept an apology. She grew angrier and angrier as Cannon spoke with her husband and did not address her directly. Hearing enough from the less-than-contrite miner, Josefa snapped and pulled a large knife from the folds of her dress.

Modern-day view of downtown Downieville with the Jersey Bridge in center. On July 5, 1851, Josefa Segovia was lynched on that spot.

She plunged the knife deep into Cannon's chest, and without a word he slumped to the ground and died. No one knows what Cannon said to provoke such violence, but Josefa later claimed she had been insulted.

Following the stabbing, Josefa, in a vain attempt to hide from the angry lynch mob that began to assemble, ran and hid at a nearby saloon. Witnesses would later describe the mob as one of the craziest and wildest ever witnessed in the region. Knowing that her situation was hopeless and that there was no escape, Josefa voluntarily surrendered to local authorities. She was placed under arrest and held under guard at an unoccupied log cabin until a hastily convened court was assembled that afternoon. As the day progressed, the large crowd grew impatient and demanded immediate justice. After a brief and biased hearing, which lasted less than an hour, a jury of twelve men found Josefa guilty of murder and sentenced her to death.

As with most miners' courts of the era, sentences were carried out immediately, and Josefa was led to a hastily erected scaffold on the Jersey Bridge that spanned the Yuba River. As she walked to her execution, she was alleged to have held her head high, not wanting to show any fear. A crowd, estimated at more than 5,000 people, stood nearby to witnesses the tragic event. On the bridge, Josefa stood emotionless and refused a blindfold. When asked if she had any last words, she allegedly nodded and simply said, "Adiós señores." A noose was placed around her neck, and at the sound of a pistol shot, her body was flung over the edge of the bridge.

Josefa Segovia was the first and only woman to be lynched in the state of California. Following her execution, wild rumors began to circulate that she might have been pregnant at the time. This legend has persisted into modern times but has never been proven. Segovia's body was left to hang on the bridge for several hours after her execution and was eventually given to friends for burial.

In a cruel twist of fate, Josefa and Fred Cannon were buried beside one another on a hill at the Downieville Cemetery.

The Lady in Black
LAURA FAIR
(1870, San Francisco)

On the afternoon of November 3, 1870, an attractive thirty-three-year-old woman clad in a black cloak and veil paced the decks of the *El Capitan*, an Oakland–San Francisco-bound ferry, anxiously looking for someone. On the upper deck of the ship, she found the person she was looking for: a middle-aged well-to-do man sitting between a plump middle-aged woman and a teenage boy. The woman stared intently at the family from the shadows, and in a momentary flash of rage stepped toward the family, pulled a four-shot Derringer pistol from her cloak, took aim, and shot the man in the chest. She then dropped the weapon and simply walked away. Thus began one of the most sensational and bizarre crime stories of the nineteenth century: the Fair-Crittenden murder case.

Alexander Parker Crittenden was born on January 14, 1816, in Lexington, Kentucky. His family was well-connected, and his father was a close friend of former President Andrew Jackson. Through these political connections, Crittenden was able to secure an appointment to the United States Military Academy at West Point from which he graduated in 1836. Two years later he married, moved to Texas, and became a lawyer. In 1849, like so many other fortune-seekers, he and his family traveled to California. Crittenden settled in San Francisco, opened a successful law practice, and was elected to two terms in the California Assembly (1850 and 1852). After leaving office, he returned to San Francisco and renewed his law practice. In 1863, he ventured to Virginia City, Nevada, following the discovery of silver. While there, he met and became infatuated with a pretty twenty-six-year-old boardinghouse owner named Laura Fair, and the two began a lurid seven-year affair.

Laura Fair, mistress of Alexander Parker Crittenden; she shot and killed him aboard the ferry boat *El Capitan* in 1870. *Courtesy University of Nevada, Reno.*

Laura Hunt-Fair was born in Alabama in 1837, and from an early age her life was filled with marital uncertainties and unstable financial conditions. At the age of sixteen, she married a New Orleans liquor wholesaler, who died less than a year after the nuptials. She was subsequently married two more times, to Thomas Gracien (divorced) and to William Fair (who committed suicide in 1861, and with whom she had one daughter). For a brief period in the early 1860s, she was an actress and appeared at the Metropolitan Theater in Sacramento. With money she saved from this and other ventures, she moved to Virginia City and purchased a boardinghouse just as the Comstock Lode was discovered.

Upon arrival in Virginia City, in 1864, Crittenden booked lodging at the Tahoe House, owned by Laura Fair. Upon meeting the beautiful boardinghouse proprietor, he was immediately smitten. The sexual attraction was mutual. They soon began a torrid love affair. At first, Laura wasn't aware of her lover's marital status, but in early 1865, she learned the truth when Crittenden's wife, Clara, and their children arrived in Virginia City. Understandably upset, Laura foolishly believed his promises to leave his wife and marry her very soon. He then rented a house for his family but secretly kept a room at the Tahoe House. Crittenden would spend time at both places, selfishly unwilling to give up his family or his mistress. Variations of this illicit arrangement would continue in Virginia City and San Francisco for the next five years.

In 1870, the Crittendens permanently moved back to San Francisco, and Alexander's affair with Laura Fair began to wane. The lovers argued frequently, and eventually she gave up and married another man, Jesse Snyder. When Alexander found out, he was furious; the thought of his lover with another man drove him crazy. In desperation, he wrote Laura a letter detailing his devotion, enduring love, and determination to legitimize their relationship with marriage. The letter worked, and Laura agreed to a reconciliation. The lovers both vowed to seek divorces from their spouses, but only Laura followed through.

Laura's divorce became final on October 5, 1870, and ironically, on the very same day, Mrs. Crittenden traveled east to be with family. Laura assumed naively that she and Alexander were finally going to be together forever. The

Modern-day photo of the Tahoe House Hotel, Virginia City, Nevada.

Stereoscopic view of ferry boat *El Capitan*, at the Terminus. *Courtesy of the Miriam and Ira D. Wallach Division of Art, Prints and Photographs: Photography Collection, New York Public Library.*

situation began to sour quickly, though, when she discovered Alexander had not asked his wife for a divorce prior to her departure. She finally realized the relationship was never going to change, and something inside of her snapped. Laura purchased a four-shot Derringer pistol.

On the afternoon of November 3, 1870, Crittenden went to Oakland to greet his wife and children upon their return home at the train station. The family rode by carriage to the Oakland pier and boarded the *El Capitan* for the short ferry ride across the bay to San Francisco. The whole time, Laura Fair, heavily veiled and wearing a black dress, had been watching the happy reunion, and her anger was reaching a boiling point. Once the Crittenden family had found seats on the boat, Fair decided to act and hurried toward the family. She pulled out the Derringer revolver and shot Alexander in the chest. He slumped to the floor of the boat, and Fair attempted to escape but was quickly apprehended by members of the ferry's crew and placed under arrest. For nearly two days, Crittenden lay mortally wounded, and on November 5, he finally succumbed to his injuries.

Laura Fair was charged with first-degree murder, and during her sensational trial, which began in April 1871, she admitted to having a long-term affair with Crittenden. She tearfully testified that he had continually told her that he would divorce his wife and marry her. She also stated that she had no recollection of ever pulling the trigger. The defense maintained that she suffered from mental instability due to delayed menstruation cycles, which ultimately led her to kill her estranged lover. They went on to describe Alexander Crittenden's deceit and betrayal as the cause of Fair's blind rage when she shot him.

On April 26, 1871, after deliberating for only forty minutes, the jury found Fair guilty of first-degree murder. On June 3, she was officially sentenced to death by hanging and was the first woman in California to legally receive the death penalty. On July 11, the California State Supreme Court vacated the conviction on procedural issues and ordered a new trial. Her second trial began on September 17, 1872, and it was far less sensational than the first. After less than two weeks of testimony and jury deliberation, Fair was found not guilty by reason of insanity and released.

After the end of her ordeal, Laura Fair wrote a book called *Wolves in the Fold*, in which she criticized the prosecution and the press. She also popped up as a character in Mark Twain's novel *The Gilded Age*. She married for a fifth time and then faded into history, eking out a meager living in various mining camps of Eureka Valley. Her daughter, Lillian Hollis, was a celebrated beauty and successful stage actress who died in semi-squalid conditions on February 3, 1913, in New York City. Laura Fair-Snyder died from heart failure on October 13, 1919, alone in her tiny apartment on Market Street in San Francisco, aged eighty-two, and was buried at Woodlawn Cemetery in Colma, California.

A Virtuous Woman
Turns to Murder
LASTENIA ABARTA
(1881, Los Angeles)

Francisco "Chico" Forster was the dynamic forty-year-old son of John "Don Juan" Forster, one of early California's largest and most influential landowners. His maternal uncle Pio Pico was the last Mexican governor of Alta, California. Chico was one of Los Angeles's most eligible bachelors but developed a nasty reputation as a scoundrel and womanizer. On an early spring day in 1881, Chico's callous disregard for women finally caught up with him when his most recent lover, Lastenia Abarta, ended his life on a busy street corner of the city. What followed shocked residents of Los Angeles, and during Abarta's sensational three-week murder trial, defense attorneys presented forensic evidence and scientific testimony of their client's innocence by reason of "impulsive insanity due to female issues."

Pio Pico, last Mexican Governor of Alta California, circa 1870. *Courtesy of the Anaheim Public Library.*

Very little is known about Lastenia Abarta's early life, and even less is known about her life after the Forster tragedy. What *is* known is that she was born in Los Angeles, around 1863, the daughter of French immigrant Pierre "Pedro" Abarta and Ysabel Rada. As a teenager she was known as one of the most beautiful and talented singers in the city. After her father's death in 1877, she began singing in area dance halls to help support the family.

Chico Forster met Lastenia in September 1878, and in the three years prior to the shooting he was a constant visitor at the Abarta residence and made numerous honorable propositions of marriage, but he never made good on any of his promises. On the early evening of Friday, March 10, 1881, Forster arrived at Abarta's home, produced a marriage license,

Modern-day photo of the Plaza Church in Los Angeles.

and persuaded Lastenia to elope with him. They rode around the city for several hours in a vain attempt at finding someone to marry them. Undaunted, Forster persuaded Lastenia to accompany him to the Moiso Mansion House, where he would procure a room and continue the search for a priest in the morning. The couple stayed at the hotel for the next two days and apparently had sexual relations. On Sunday morning, increasingly anxious over losing her virginity, Abarta spent hours holed up in the hotel room, waiting in vain for Forster to return with a priest to perform the marriage ceremony. The next day, knowing that her reputation and virtue had been destroyed, she left the hotel and returned home. That same day she purchased a small handgun, and over the next two days contemplated suicide.

On Wednesday morning, March 15, Hortensia Abarta found her older sister sitting in the parlor of their home, crying and holding a gun in her lap. Lastenia told her the heart-wrenching details of Forster's betrayal and that she wanted to die. Hortensia persuaded Lastenia to accompany her in a vain attempt to locate her reluctant beau and make the situation right. After several hours of searching the city, they found him at Covarrubias's stable.

After a brief but heated conversation, he agreed to accompany them to the Plaza Church for a wedding. Along the way, Forster had a change of heart, stopped the carriage at the corner of Commercial and Los Angeles Streets, and got out. Both women followed, and after arguing for several minutes, Lastenia pulled a revolver from her skirt pocket and shot him once

Guildford Wiley Wells, former congressmen and defense attorney. *Courtesy of the Library of Congress. Prints and Photographs Division. Brady-Handy Collection. LC-BH832-29282.*

in the right eye, killing him instantly. She attempted to fire another shot but was restrained by a bystander. She then calmly walked several blocks to the office of Judge Trafford and surrendered. She was arrested and charged with first-degree murder.

Abarta's murder trial began on April 28, before Superior Court Judge Ygnacio Sepulveda. Defending her were two of the city's most prominent criminal defense attorneys, Guilford Wiley Wells, a former Mississippi congressmen and consul in Shanghai, and John F. Godfrey, a former Los Angeles city attorney. Together they saw a way to an acquittal that others thought impossible. Prosecutors argued that the slaying of Forster had been premeditated, and the motive was revenge. The defense argued that the defendant had been driven to kill because of medical issues and shame.

During the nineteenth century, the American medical establishment was dominated by men who harbored an obsession with what was commonly referred to as "female hysteria." Medical journals of the time linked this syndrome to sexual deprivation and the influences of an oversexed uterus. By the 1880s, many physicians believed that female hysteria was an epidemic.

It was in this climate of mistaken medical beliefs that Abarta's lawyers sought to build their case. A long stream of medical experts took the stand, most agreeing that female hysteria was a uterine disorder brought about by irregular menstrual periods that often affected the female's mental state. But it was the testimony of Dr. Joseph Kurtz, a local physician that sealed the jurors' decision. He stated that he had seen the defendant regularly over the past several years and that she suffered from suppressed menstruation, and that upon recent examination it was also determined that she was no longer a virgin. He went on to give detailed testimony on the different impulsive mental disorders associated with irregular menstruation cycles that, in his expert opinion, had driven Lastenia Abarta to lose her reasoning ability and commit homicide. On the morning of Monday, May 2, after three days of testimony, the all-male jury deliberated for twenty minutes before deciding to acquit Abarta of the murder charges.

Forster family crypt at the Old Mission Cemetery in San Juan Capistrano, California.

In the aftermath of the tragedy and less than a year after his favorite son's death, a depressed and disheartened Don Juan Forster died and was buried beside his son in the family mausoleum at the Old Mission Cemetery in San Juan Capistrano. In January 1883, Lastenia Abarta married Augustin Cazuax in Los Angeles and then disappeared into the pages of history.

The She-Devil
HATTIE WOOLSTEEN
(1887, Los Angeles)

In the late evening of October 7, 1887, an empty barn near Compton belonging to a widow named Emeline Barbey was found on fire. The following day, a thorough search of the burned-out building uncovered the charred remains of an unknown male. There was talk of foul play, but no concrete evidence yet existed. On the body was found a pin, a pair of sleeve buttons, and portions of suit cloth (which had been doused in coal oil) that might help identify the body.

In the preceding week, Dr. Charles N. Harlan, a prominent Los Angeles dentist had gone missing. Besides being a dentist, Harlan was also a known gambler who often associated with criminal and unscrupulous characters. Police quickly began to suspect that the charred remains found on the Barbey farm might belong to the missing dentist. Portions of the cloth were taken to the McConnell & Company tailor shop on North Spring Street in downtown Los Angeles. They were able to positively identify the cloth pieces as coming from a suit that was owned by Charles Harlan. On October 13, an autopsy and dental examination of the body positively identified the remains as belonging to Harlan. Because of the condition of the body, it was impossible to determine whether there were any signs of violence.

HATTIE WOOLSTEEN.

This portrait of Hattie Woolsteen appeared in the 1888 edition of *Defenders and Offenders*, Buchner & Company, New York.

Detectives were baffled as to how Harlan ended up in Compton, for he had no known business or acquaintances in the area. But they soon began to speculate that Harlan had most likely been killed because of a gambling dispute, his body taken to Compton, and the barn set ablaze to hide the evidence of the crime. As quickly as this theory evolved, it was swiftly dismissed when investigators became aware of a young, attractive twenty-two-year-old woman named Hattie Woolsteen. She had been the last person to see Harlan alive.

Hattie and her younger sister, Minnie Woolsteen, had left Peoria, Illinois, in 1886, after a brief brush with the law. Their father, Henry, had paid several hundred dollars to free them from jail, where they had been confined for allegedly stealing a watch from a jeweler. Arriving in Los Angeles the following year, both women began working as servants for a prominent family before moving into a boardinghouse on South Fort Street. In February 1887, experiencing dental problems, Hattie visited the dental office of Dr. Charles Harlan on Spring Street. Harlan was immediately infatuated with the tall, beautiful blonde, and the sexual attraction was mutual. They soon began dating, and a steamy but tumultuous love affair ensued. Hattie was unaware that he was a married man.

On October 14, Los Angeles Police Chief Patrick Darcy brought both Hattie and her sister, Minnie, in for questioning. Police detectives were alerted to the fact that Hattie and Harlan had hired a buggy on the early evening of October 7, at the livery stable on the corner of Hill and Fourth Streets in Los Angeles. The following morning, the buggy was returned by Woolsteen alone.

Hattie initially denied any involvement in the murder, and when she requested a lawyer, Chief Darcy allegedly answered, "Damn you, I'm lawyer enough for you." He later denied making the statement. The following day, she provided a variety of sketchy scenarios regarding how Harlan had most likely died. Initially she stated that she had been with Harlan the day before his body was discovered but denied being involved. Pressed further, she stated that Harlan, in a despondent state of mind, had actually killed himself after she refused to go with him to Denver. Fearing that the sound of the gunshot would draw attention and that she would be held responsible, she decided to hide the body in Emeline Barbey's barn.

Unconvinced that Hattie was a hapless witness to a suicide, police pressed further, and the story changed yet again when she stated that after her refusal to move to Denver, he pulled a revolver from his pocket and said that one of them must die. She begged him not to shoot her, and a struggle for the weapon ensued. It discharged, accidentally striking Harlan in the head. Her story changed many times, and police detectives knew she was rehearsing.

She looked them straight in the eye and with a devilish grin said, "Which one is the most likely to tell effectively in court?" Unmoved by Hattie's denials and ever-changing story, police arrested her and charged her with Harlan's murder.

Within a week, Hattie's case was a media sensation with rumors and innuendo swirling around the case. Stories abounded, including the preposterous possibility that the body found at the Barbey barn was not Charles Harlan and that he had actually fled the state because of gambling debt. It was also scandalously alleged that while in custody, Woolsteen had been sexually harassed by jailers and even by the chief of police. In private circles, it was whispered that the Woolsteen sisters were con artists with a long history of criminal activities stretching from Illinois to the West Coast. During the proceedings, the public was held spellbound by titillating headlines that were splashed across newspapers in the region. Local newspapers dubbed Hattie "Wicked Woolsteen," "The Fiendish Murderess," and "The She-Devil."

In mid-October, shortly after her arraignment, Hattie attempted suicide by ingesting a large quantity of chloroform. Quick aid from jail physicians saved her life. The image of Woolsteen as a grief-stricken lover struck a chord with the public, and soon powerful women's rights advocates rallied to her defense. They began regarding her as a victim of gender inequality and helped fund her defense along with her faithful father, Henry. Defending Hattie were two of Los Angeles's most respected and high-powered attorneys, G. Wiley Wells and soon-to-be United States Senator Stephen M. White.

On April 2, after five months of delays, Hattie's murder trial finally began before Judge William Cheney. By this time the police chief had been fired, and the media was now sympathizing with Hattie, calling the case "a tale of a young girl's sorrow and a man's lustful brutality." Throughout the two-week trial, Hattie remained stoic and unemotional, often wearing a black dress and matching veil that covered her face.

Prosecutors claimed that the beautiful temptress had lured her lover into a barn, shot and robbed him, set fire to the building, and then buried the gun and his watch, taking with her his diamond ring, a locket, and some cash. Her motive was revenge for seducing her and failing to make good on his marriage proposal. Defense attorneys claimed Harlan was a habitual gambler in serious debt, an unfaithful husband who was sexually out of control, and a charlatan who boasted of drugging other female patients before taking his pleasure with them—including the defendant, whom he had pursued with gifts and false promises of love and marriage.

The prosecution's case was built primarily on circumstantial evidence, and they made some serious blunders, including calling Horace Shinn to the witness stand. Shinn was a close friend of the victim and fellow dentist, who testified that in the weeks leading up to Harlan's death the deceased had boasted of his sexual conquests and escapades with the defendant and many other women. This information only bolstered the defense's argument that Harlan was a scoundrel and philanderer. On April 9, a shocking turn of events took place when Woolsteen's confession and other comments given to police were deemed inadmissible because police investigators had used coercive tactics to elicit the confession. This was a serious blow to the prosecution's already flimsy circumstantial case.

On April 12, Woolsteen took the witness stand in her own defense and testified that she had first met Dr. Harlan in February 1887, when she had some dental work done at his office. She stated that he created a story about a decaying tooth, sedated her, and took improper sexual liberties. Greatly distressed by this, she went to visit a friend, Mrs. Barbey, at her Compton farm. Harlan pursued her, and, smitten with the handsome and debonair doctor, she soon forgave him for his indiscretions, hoping that everything would end in marriage. She went on to state that in July, Harlan had proposed marriage, but she denied under oath that she was aware he was already married. Three months later she told the court that she found out he had been seeing other women. When she asked him about this, he broke down and confessed all of his misbehavior and begged for forgiveness.

On the day of the shooting, unable to endure the disappointment, she bought a handgun with the intent to kill herself. When Harlan called on her that evening and asked to take a ride and talk, she reluctantly agreed. With her gun tucked inside her handbag, she and Harlan set out on a buggy ride to the vacant Barbey farm on Lemon Street (now Compton Boulevard), which Harlan said he wanted to buy for her. Along the way, she insisted that the relationship was over and that this would be the last time they would ever go out. When they reached the Barbey farm, Harlan got out and insisted that the horses needed rest and that they needed to stay the night. Protesting, Woolsteen stated that she asked what his true intentions were, but before she could utter another word, he attacked her and threw her into a stack of hay. Reaching for the revolver in the pocket of her coat, she insisted that her objective was to harm herself rather than submit sexually to a man she now detested. When she pointed the gun at her own heart, Harlan attempted to wrestle the gun away, and it discharged accidentally, fatally striking him in the head. She then stated that before returning to Los Angeles, she stopped at an isolated spot near the intersection of West 8th Street and Garland Avenue and buried the gun and Harlan's other belongings. She stated that she had no recollection why she had done that or how the barn caught fire.

On the late afternoon of April 14, the jury began deliberating Woolsteen's fate. Ten minutes later came the shocking announcement that the jury had reached a verdict. As the jury filed in, all eyes were upon them, as spectators endeavored to gain an idea as to the nature of the speedy verdict. From the shortness of the time they had been out, it was evident that no compromise verdict would be rendered, and most onlookers certainly felt the defendant would be found not guilty. The defendant, surrounded by her lawyers, sat nervously as the jury foreman stood and stoically read the verdict: "We, the jury, find the defendant, Hattie Woolsteen, not guilty of the charge of murder." The announcement was greeted with an outburst of applause, which was quickly suppressed by officers of the court. Above the chaos, Judge Cheney ordered Woolsteen's immediate release from custody. The jubilant crowd slowly filed out of the courtroom and gathered in the hallway, where they waited for Woolsteen to appear. When she finally emerged, the crowd greeted her with thunderous cheers. Following her acquittal, Hattie and her sister returned to Peoria, Illinois, and resumed a quiet life away from the glaring newspaper headlines.

Why did the murder of a philandering dentist captivate the public? The answer can be found in Victorian ideas of class, gender, and sexuality. During the nineteenth century many people believed that murder was a crime committed exclusively by men, and women were most often portrayed as the victims. Hattie Woolsteen admitted in court that she had killed her lover but declared it a tragic accident, which was just one of many confusing explanations. Did Hattie Woolsteen get away with murder? No one knows for sure, but examination of the evidence does cast suspicion in her direction. In the end, though, nothing involving this tragedy was perfectly clear.

A Battered Woman
ISABELLA ANDROSS
(1887, San Pedro)

B attered woman syndrome: A woman who has been repeatedly subjected to any forceful physical or psychological behavior by a man in order to coerce her to do something he wants her to do without any concern for her rights may suffer from BWS.

While sailing under the flag of Spain, Portuguese explorer Juan Rodriguez Cabrillo was the first European to set eyes upon the barren hills and plains of what was to be Rancho San Pedro. On October 8, 1542, he sailed into the bay and noticed several wildfires burning in the surrounding hills, producing dark plumes of smoke. He named the area *Bahia de los Fumos*, which was Spanish for "Bay of Smokes." Regular settlement began in 1769, as part of the effort to populate California, although trade restrictions encouraged more smuggling than regular, more legitimate, business. When Mexico won its independence, these trade limitations were lifted, and the town began to flourish. Over the next one hundred years, San Pedro became one of the most important ports on the Pacific Coast and, like San Francisco's Barbary Coast, gained a reputation for its debauchery that attracted all sorts of unsavory characters, both male and female.

December 12, 1887, was a very busy day for the Los Angeles County coroner. On that day there were four inquests into suspicious deaths within the county. One case involved the stabbing death of a former merchant seaman in San Pedro, California. Around 11:30 p.m. on December 10, Deputy Constable John T. Hogan was notified that Henry Neidman, twenty-seven, had been badly injured from a stab wound at Brown's dance hall and saloon. The establishment, like many other similar businesses in the area, was a notorious hangout for unpleasant characters who liked to drink, gamble, socialize with women of questionable virtue, and cause lots of mayhem.

When Constable Hogan arrived on the scene, he found Neidman dead in the entranceway of the saloon, lying in a pool of his own blood. The deceased had sustained a massive stab wound to the groin and had bled to death before help could arrive. Witnesses told the officer that Isabella Andross—a twenty-something beauty of Mexican descent, the mother of a young boy, and girlfriend of the deceased—had allegedly committed the crime and was hiding in her room upstairs at the saloon. When Hogan confronted Andross, she immediately confessed to killing Neidman and requested to be taken directly to jail for her own safety.

A search of the premises uncovered a dress owned by Andross, which was sprinkled with fresh blood, and the murder weapon was located on a dressing bureau. Police also discovered a trail of blood that led directly from Andross's room back to the deceased. Although Isabella initially confessed that she had killed Neidman, she changed her story and denied any involvement in the slaying. She told investigators that no one had seen her do it, and they'd have to prove she was responsible. A coroner's inquest convened the next day and found that there was sufficient evidence to charge Andross with Neidman's murder, and she was bound over for trial. During her incarceration at the Los Angeles County jail, Isabella was instrumental in saving the life of another accused murderess. On April 14, 1888, Andross alerted jailers to the attempted suicide of Hattie Woolsteen, who was accused of killing her lover. Woolsteen had attempted to choke herself to death with a shawl.

After several months of delays, Andross's murder trial began on May 4. As the jury entered the courtroom, the heavily veiled defendant sat calm and emotionless next to her defense attorney. Her young son sat in the courtroom gallery a few feet behind his mother, oblivious to the significance of the proceedings that were about to unfold. The prosecution called several witnesses, including employees of the saloon and acquaintances of both the defendant and the deceased. They testified that they had witnessed a quarrel between the two at another dance hall on the night of the slaying but were unaware of the cause of the argument. One witness stated that Neidman tried to avoid the squabble by leaving the saloon but was followed by the defendant. It was learned that both parties had been drinking heavily on the night of the murder. Other prosecution witnesses included physicians and police officers associated with the case.

On May 5, an emotional Andross took the witness stand in her own defense and acknowledged that she had been married but that her husband had abandoned the family for another woman several years prior. She went on to testify that she had met the deceased at Brown's dance hall shortly after her husband had left and that she was employed as a part-time seamstress. Neidman worked as a bartender at the dance hall. Andross admitted that they soon became lovers and began living together at the dance hall.

She stated that Neidman was, at first, sweet and kind but after several weeks became emotionally abusive. Needing money, he suggested that she take other men into her "confidence," and what that actually meant can only be assumed to be sexual in nature. Andross admitted that she reluctantly agreed to his indecent proposition, fearing she had no other options. Soon Neidman stopped working altogether, and they both depended on her meager income from prostitution and seamstress duties. He required that she turn over all her earnings and then promptly squandered it all on gambling. She stated that this arrangement went on for several years, during which time they continued to live together on and off.

On the night of the slaying, Andross alleged that she and a girlfriend had visited another dance hall, where she discovered Neidman dancing and flirting with another woman. In a jealous rage, she angrily confronted him. Unfazed by her anger, Neidman fired back several vulgar expletives and retreated to the bar area. This enraged Andross even more, and she followed. The fight continued all the way back to Brown's dance hall. Once at the dance hall, Neidman forcefully attempted to take her to their room, but she told him to leave and that she wanted to end the relationship. He then slapped her face and grabbed her wrist. Afraid for her safety, she broke free, and Neidman, in close pursuit, grabbed her hair and flung her to the ground outside of the dance hall. He began choking her, yelled "I'll kill you tonight," and hit her several more times in the face. Fearing for her life, she pulled a knife from the folds of her dress and slashed wildly in an attempt to escape the clutches of her attacker. Neidman, mortally injured, immediately let go and slumped to the ground. Andross stated she then ran to her room and waited for police to arrive. She also testified that she did not know how many times she had actually stabbed Neidman or where the wounds were located. She went on to say that when Constable Hogan arrived on the scene, she made several incriminating statements that weren't true in order to escape the angry mob that had formed outside the saloon. Although she confessed to stabbing Neidman, she did it because she feared her life was in danger; there was no intent to kill.

On May 7, after two days of grueling testimony, Andross was excused from the witness stand, and the defense rested its case. Later that same evening the all-male jury began deliberating Andross's fate, and after only a few hours of discussion, they reached a unanimous decision. Judge William A. Cheney was alerted and convened the court the following morning. At 11:00 a.m. the jurors filed into the courtroom without a sound. None of them showed the slightest emotion as to how they had voted. The defendant sat nearby nervously staring straight ahead. The verdict was handed to the judge, who then handed the envelope to the court clerk, who stood and read, "We, the jury, in the case of the People v. Isabella Andross charged with murder of Henry Neidman of San Pedro, find the defendant not guilty."

The packed courtroom erupted into chaos. Andross's emotions boiled over, and she began to sob uncontrollably with her hands on her face. She was comforted by her attorney and friends. As she confidently exited the courthouse, tears of relief streamed down her face. Holding the hand of her young son, she quietly and proudly walked away from the courthouse a free woman. She was never to be heard from again.

An Abusive Husband Gets His Just Rewards

BRIDGET WATERS

(1888, Los Angeles)

Domestic violence against women, particularly married women, was a prominent occurrence in Victorian times. It was generally perceived to be socially acceptable and was prevalent in all classes. These assaults were mainly attributed to the idea that the man was the ruler of his home. Domestic principles of the era promoted the dominance of men, and it was considered a husband's duty to protect his wife, but in contradiction this also allowed for him to use violence to keep her in line if necessary.

In the area of religion, it was suggested that for a woman to be virtuous and serve God, she must follow the lead of her husband, which then gave men the impression that they had a God-given right to control their wives, even if that meant the use of physical correction. Due to the fact that religion was claimed to be an important Victorian ideal, men believed that for a woman to lead a virtuous life, they had to follow the wishes of their husbands— even if those wishes allowed her to be beaten.

In the courtroom, a husband had legal power over most of his wife's possessions, including her property, wages, children, and any inheritance. Because of this, many women felt enslaved to their husbands. The relationship of a wife and husband was commonly compared to that of a slave and his master. The informal traditions of the Victorian era allowed a man to be overbearing and, if necessary, physically violent with his wife in order to protect her rights and, in an absurd rationalization, the woman's rights as well.

Men often casually justified this violence, and most women reluctantly accepted it as a way of life. The ideals concerning law, religion, and domestic roles contributed to allowing spousal abuse. But in the later nineteenth century, women did gain some rights through reform laws that allowed them child custody and possession of their own things. Complaints of domestic violence against women, particularly wives, during Victorian times were generally only taken seriously in sporadic instances. In certain circumstances, few and far between, some women felt compelled to take the law into their own hands, often with deadly consequences. The following case is one such instance.

Around 6:00 p.m. on the evening of May 1, 1888, Los Angeles City Patrol Officer Patrick Martin was walking his beat in the San Fernando Street neighborhood of the city when he was approached by Mrs. Bridget Waters, the caretaker of a local boardinghouse. In an agitated state, she told the officer that her estranged husband, Peter Waters, had just arrived in town. Previously, he had made several attempts on her life, and because of this she was forced to flee her home in Oakland four months prior. She told the officer that she feared for her life, had been constantly on the move, and was certain he would find out where she was living. She also stated that a warrant had been issued for his arrest in connection with several prior threats of violence that occurred in the San Francisco Bay area. Officer Martin expressed his concern and promised Mrs. Waters that he would look for her husband.

An hour later, unsuccessful in locating Peter Waters, Officer Martin was returning to the boardinghouse where Mrs. Waters resided when he heard a gunshot that appeared to emanate from the boardinghouse. Before he could reach the home, another shot rang out, and he witnessed a man tumble out the front door and fall to the sidewalk. Two additional gunshots followed. The officer quickly determined that the stricken man was Peter Waters. He had been shot multiple times by his wife, who was now standing over the injured man with the still-smoking pistol in her hand. Carefully approaching the scene, Officer Martin promptly disarmed the woman, who tearfully pleaded with the officer to return the weapon so she could finish the job.

The wounded man was taken to a local hospital, where he was not expected to live through the night. He told police investigators that he had gone to his wife's home in an ill-advised attempt at reconciling their relationship and had no intent of doing any harm. Shortly after this statement, Mrs. Waters was placed under arrest and charged with attempted murder. Later that evening, Peter Waters succumbed to his injuries without giving any further statements. The charges against Mrs. Waters were immediately elevated to murder, and because she was unable to raise the $10,000 bail needed to get out on bond, she remained in custody at the city jail.

She did not deny shooting her husband and insisted that she had done it in self-defense. She showed no remorse and told police investigators that during their entire marriage her husband had treated her like a slave. He not only beat her regularly but was also emotionally abusive. Fearing for the safety of her children, she felt compelled to flee northern California but was

The old Los Angeles County Courthouse, 1861–1891. *Courtesy of the Security Pacific National Bank Collection/ Los Angeles Public Library.*

stalked from place to place by her husband. She settled in Los Angeles four months prior to the tragedy and found employment at the boardinghouse where the shooting took place. She said that on the day of the murder she became hysterical when she learned that her husband was in the city and vowed to do whatever it took to keep him away. So when he came to her home on that terrible night, she felt there was no other option than to take justice into her own hands. She needed to free herself once and for all from her tormentor.

Bridget Waters's murder trial began on June 1, and would last less than a week. During the proceedings, numerous witnesses collaborated Mrs. Waters's claims of years of domestic violence at the hands of her husband. On June 5, Carrie Anselmo, Mrs. Waters's teenage daughter from a previous marriage, took the witness stand and testified that on the day of the shooting she had heard that her stepfather was back in town and was intent on killing her mother. She stated that around 7:30 p.m. she witnessed her stepfather shove his way into their home on San Fernando Street, and a quarrel soon erupted between her parents in the entrance hallway of the boardinghouse. The argument quickly turned physical when her stepfather struck the first blows upon her mother. She recalled hearing him yell, "I've got you now, and I'm going to kill you." Anselmo then witnessed him pull a handgun from his pocket, whereupon her mother screamed, "For God's sake! Don't let him kill me!" Frightened by the events, the young girl recalled running from the house to the safety of a nearby drugstore.

When Mrs. Waters began her testimony on the afternoon of June 5, she stated that she had endured nearly two years of constant abuse. On the night of the shooting, she recalled that around 7:00 p.m. she sat down with a cup of tea in the parlor of the boardinghouse and was suddenly confronted by her estranged husband. She asked him to leave, but he lunged at her, and a great struggle commenced. She told the court that she was able to free herself momentarily and witnessed him pull a pistol from his coat pocket. At that moment, compelled to save her own life, she pulled her own handgun from the folds of her dress and fired the first shot. She told the jury that she feared for her life and the safety of her children and was compelled to shoot her husband to end the attack.

On June 6, closing arguments commenced, and the toll of the trial began to show its effects on the defendant, who appeared weary and on the verge of an emotional breakdown. At 5:00 p.m. the judge ordered the jury to begin deliberations, and after only fifteen minutes returned a verdict of not guilty. The jury foreman made a brief statement that the shooting death had been justified, and Peter Waters had gotten what he deserved.

Tragedy in Tustin
EFFIE SCHOLL
(1889, Orange County)

By early October 1889, Effie J. Scholl was struggling to hold her life together. She was divorced with two young children and struggling financially, and the mental strain of the community's indignation regarding divorce was taking its toll. Although women's rights pertaining to divorce and child custody were evolving during this time, the community as a whole still frowned upon it and often ostracized women because of it. Reeling from this alienation, Effie Scholl was even further stressed by her ex-husband's attempt to gain custody of the children. She apparently had no other options, and these combined factors led her to commit an unconscionable horror. The heinous savagery and senselessness of these acts would haunt the tiny community of Tustin, California, for decades.

Effie J. Goodwin and Orr Scholl were married in Tustin, on September 28, 1883. He was a well-liked member of the community with a reputation for honesty and integrity. She was seen as being hotheaded, irrational, and emotionally unbalanced. Friends and relatives of Orr's tried to prevent the marriage due to his bride's temperament. Five years into the marriage and after having two children together, Orr Scholl filed for divorce. He had

Modern-day photo of the Tustin home of Effie Scholl, where she murdered her children on October 16, 1889.

traveled to Tuolumne County to look after his mining interests. Divorce papers were initially filed there but were eventually transferred to Los Angeles County. He cited his wife's violent temper and other cruelties as reason for the dissolution of the marriage. Effie Scholl responded by filing a cross-complaint, alleging desertion on her husband's part. A decree of absolute divorce was declared in favor of Mrs. Scholl, because her husband failed to appear at the trial and allowed the case to go against him by default. She was awarded full custody of both children.

In the year after the divorce, Orr returned to Tustin and began working at a local grocery store. Effie and the two children moved into a tiny cottage adjacent to her mother's home at the corner of Pacific and 3rd Streets. During the year since the divorce, Effie had struggled financially and was forced to seek public aid. Because of this, she was placed on the county's indigent list, which caused tremendous embarrassment and public humiliation.

Effie and Orr's relationship since the divorce was contemptuous and divisive. Neither parent ever truly thought of the children's best interests. Both parties bickered incessantly about personal matters, which only compounded Effie's unstable behavior. On October 11, 1889, Orr Scholl discovered his ex-wife had been placed on the indigent list and applied to the court for custody of his children, alleging that their mother was unfit to care for them any longer. When Effie was served with these papers, she became hysterical and vowed that she would kill herself and the children before letting her ex-husband gain control.

In the early morning hours of October 16, 1889, Effie was certain she was going to lose custody of her children. In the five days since being served with the court papers, she had suffered severe insomnia, which only compounded her instability. She decided to make good on her threats. Rationalizing that there was no other course of action, she preferred her children's deaths and her own suicide rather than suffer the humiliation of her ex-husband gaining custody. She believed the children, five-year-old John and three-year-old Eva, would be in a much better place in death rather than with her ex-husband.

As the tragic event unfolded, Effie used chloroform to subdue the children, placed them into her bed, and then slit their throats with a kitchen knife. She then ingested a

Gravesite of Effie Scholl at Santa Ana Cemetery.

bottle of carbolic acid, cut her own throat, and lost consciousness. Around 5:00 a.m., Effie's mother, who lived next door, heard strange noises coming from the cottage and investigated. Listening for a moment, she heard the stifled groans of a person in agony. Rushing to the door of the cottage and pushing it open, she beheld a horrific sight. On the bed near the door lay the semi-nude body of her daughter with a horrendous gash in her throat and her face twisted in indescribable pain. By her side were the lifeless bodies of the children. Their throats had been cut from ear to ear, and their windpipes severed so severely that it appeared there was an attempt to remove the heads from the bodies. On the bureau nearby lay two empty bottles of muriatic and carbolic acid. On the bed was found an empty bottle of chloroform, and on the floor lay the bloodstained kitchen knife. The wall beside the bed was splattered with blood three feet above the mattress.

Orr Scholl was notified of what had happened, and he hurried to the house. Transfixed by the horror of the scene, he regained enough of his senses to send for medical help, hoping there still might be time to save one of his children. When help arrived, the children were already cold with death, and their mother was writhing in deadly convulsions. When police arrived, they found a note written by Effie addressed to her mother, and it read in part: "This is the last blow of that cruel thing that calls himself a man. He can never have my sweet little ones to bring up in wickedness. I can say that he is a vile, wicked, depraved, devilish liar. My little ones will be in the arms of

Jesus. I give up life everlasting that my little ones may gain it."

Effie was moved to her mother's home next door, and the county coroner took possession of the children's bodies. Physicians did everything they could to save Effie's life, but she was not expected to survive for long. At a coroner's inquest held the next day, the jury returned a verdict of willful murder against Effie Scholl, and an arrest warrant was issued. The planned effects of the poison were not immediately successful, and Effie lingered in and out of consciousness for two more weeks. In lucid moments, she spoke with newspaper reporters and vilified her ex-husband, stating that she'd do better work of it next time should she by any chance recover. She also stated, "I don't want to live and give that man the satisfaction of seeing me hanged." In other moments she was quite repentant of the crime and had a desire to reconcile with her maker.

Around 7:00 p.m. on November 2, after eleven days of horrible suffering, Effie Scholl died. Just before taking her last breaths, she regained consciousness. Calling out to her mother and sister, she said good-bye and then quietly passed away. The following day after an autopsy and inquest, she was buried in a simple ceremony at Santa Ana Cemetery. The location of her children's graves are unknown, but they are assumed to have been laid to rest somewhere within the same cemetery.

Never Take Candy
from a Stranger
CORDELIA BOTKIN
(1898, San Francisco)

In September 1895, life for thirty-two-year-old John Preston Dunning was good. He was married to a woman he adored, he had a young daughter, and he was employed as bureau chief at the Associated Press western division office in San Francisco. He had earned a name for himself as a war correspondent years earlier while stationed in Samoa. His beautiful wife, Mary Elizabeth, age thirty-three, was the daughter of former Congressman John Brown Penington of Dover, Delaware.

On a fateful late summer day, Dunning's life would be forever changed. While strolling through Golden Gate Park near his home, he spotted an attractive woman sitting on a bench. He sat down, and they struck up a conversation. A few days later, Dunning and his new friend—Cordelia Brown-Botkin, age forty-one and a married woman who was recently separated from her husband—became lovers.

Over the next several years, they carried on their secret affair, and he was a frequent guest at her San Francisco home. During this time, Dunning began to gamble and drink heavily, and in early 1898, he was fired from his position at the Associated Press for embezzling funds to pay off gambling debts. Because he could no longer financially support his family while he searched for employment, his wife and daughter returned to Dover, Delaware, to live with her parents. Soon after his family left, Dunning moved in with Botkin at the Hotel Victoria on the corner of Bush and Stockton Streets.

Their adulterous bliss was short lived. In March 1898, Dunning was rehired by the Associated Press and accepted an assignment to cover the Spanish-American War from Cuba. At this same time he informed Cordelia that he was ending the affair. He told her he missed his wife and daughter and was going to move to Delaware after the assignment finished. She did not take the news well, and in her mind, the affair was not over.

In the summer of 1898, Mary Elizabeth Dunning began receiving anonymous letters mailed from San Francisco. These letters alleged that her husband was having an affair. On August 9, she received another mysterious note, which was signed, "With love to yourself and baby —Mrs. C." Included with the note was a small box of chocolates. After dinner, Mary Elizabeth, her older sister Ida Deane, and several others guests ate some of the chocolate. Several hours later, all became violently ill with severe stomach pain. On August 11, two days after eating the chocolates, Ida Deane died, and the next day Mary Elizabeth passed away. All the other guests recovered. Both women had suffered extremely painful and agonizing deaths, and the presumed cause was cholera, a common illness of the period. John Dunning was telegraphed about what had happened and came home right away. Once shown the letters, he immediately recognized the handwriting as that of his former lover, Cordelia Botkin. John Penington, suspecting that his daughters had been poisoned, had some of the remaining candy analyzed by a chemist who reported that some of the remaining chocolates had been spiked with arsenic. The discovery of the poison prompted a coroner's inquest, which ultimately ruled that the two women's deaths had been caused by arsenic poisoning.

Although the deaths had occurred in Delaware, law enforcement authorities requested that the case be handled by the San Francisco Police Department. After a short investigation, police were convinced that they knew who had sent the poison. Their main suspect was Cordelia Botkin, and detectives were certain that she would confess to the murders if arrested. On August 26, police confronted her at her sister's home in Sonoma County and placed her under arrest. Because she declared her innocence and did not confess, investigators were forced to solve the case by other means. They traced the origin of the arsenic to a drugstore on Market Street in San Francisco, where the pharmacist remembered selling a bottle in early June to a woman who closely matched the description of Cordelia Botkin.

Several friends of Botkin told police that they had conversations with her regarding the effects of different poisons on the body, including arsenic. Detectives searched Botkin's room at the Hotel Victoria and found wrapping paper bearing a gold seal and a company trademark that had enclosed the poisoned candy, and from this they learned that the chocolates had been purchased from the George Haas & Sons candy store on Market Street. A sales clerk at the store stated that a recent customer did fit the description of Cordelia Botkin.

To identify the person who had addressed the mailed package and penned the anonymous letters, police employed several handwriting experts, who compared samples of Botkin's writing with the anonymous letters and found they matched. But there was one problem: Not all of the candy in the box had been spiked with arsenic, and there had been no autopsies performed on the deceased, thus there was no direct proof that Dunning and Deane had actually died from arsenic poisoning.

Faced with these obstacles, detectives believed they still had a strong but circumstantial case against Botkin. Extradition papers were sent from Delaware, but Botkin's lawyer presented evidence that jurisdiction for the case was in California. In October 1898, California's Supreme Court ruled that the case would be tried in California, because Botkin's flight from Delaware was "not actual, but constructive."

The evidence was presented to the San Francisco grand jury, and on October 28, they returned an indictment charging Cordelia Botkin with two counts of first-degree murder. Her murder trial began on December 9, before Judge Carroll Cook, and on the first day of the sensational proceedings hundreds of spectators lined up outside to get a possible glimpse of the event. The trial would last several weeks, and during this time numerous witnesses were called to testify. The prosecution put John Dunning on the stand, and he admitted having an affair with the defendant and many other women. But after refusing to name these other women, he was held in contempt of court, and he served a couple days in jail before the question was withdrawn by prosecutors.

Prosecutors called several handwriting experts, who highlighted the similarities of the defendant's writing and that on the note. The defense knew that if they could not repudiate these claims, Botkin's guilt was certain. Faced with the evidence, the defense was forced to place Cordelia Botkin on the witness stand. She did not deny that she had purchased arsenic and explained that she had used the poison to clean a straw hat. The rest of her testimony

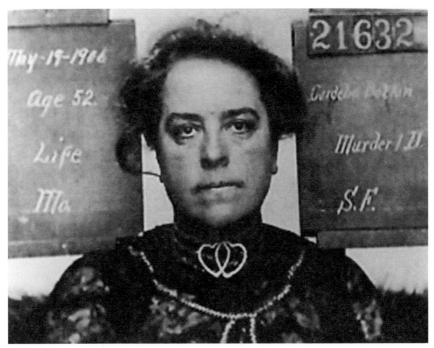

San Quentin Prison booking photo of Cordelia Botkin, 1906. *Courtesy of the Delaware Public Archives: Delaware Heritage Collection.*

produced denials of having ever been in Haas's candy store and additional flimsy alibis that could not be corroborated. Following her testimony, the defense rested its case.

On December 30, after deliberating for only four hours, the jury returned a guilty verdict of two counts of first-degree murder. The jurors had spent most of their time debating whether to recommend the death sentence or life in prison. In the end, they decided to spare her life and recommended life in prison. Throughout the entire proceedings, Botkin remained calm and showed little emotion. She could have been sent to San Quentin Prison to serve her sentence, but Judge Cook was concerned about her safety and instead ordered her to serve the sentence at the county jail in San Francisco.

Three months after the conclusion of the trial, Judge Cook was riding in his carriage in downtown San Francisco when his attention was drawn to an attractive woman whom he appeared to recognize. To his amazement he realized he was staring at Cordelia Botkin. Before he could figure out whether Botkin had escaped from prison, the woman vanished from sight. When he went to the county jail to find out whether his eyes had been deceiving him, he witnessed Botkin stroll through the front gates. He later determined that she had charmed several guards and had been afforded numerous luxuries such as an enhanced cell, special meals and clothing, unlimited access to visitors, and occasional unsupervised excursions outside of the jail.

Botkin's conviction was appealed on procedural issues and was eventually overturned by the California State Supreme Court. In March 1904, a second trial was convened, and once again on the strength of the evidence she was convicted and sentenced to life in prison. In May 1906, after the Great San Francisco Earthquake destroyed the county jail where she was serving her sentence, Botkin's days of special treatment came to an end when she was transferred to San Quentin Prison. In the coming years, unable to adjust to restrictive prison life and coupled with the deaths of her sister, son, ex-husband, and former lover John Dunning, Cordelia became depressed, and her health rapidly declined. On March 7, 1910, she died from what was described as "softening of the brain, due to melancholy." Her body was claimed by relatives and buried at Oak Mound Cemetery in Healdsburg, California.

Brutal Bride
KATIE COOK
(1899, Orange County)

In the late 1890s, in the wealthy peat lands of Orange County, California, twenty-seven-year-old Catherine "Katie" Pope married Thomas J. Cook, the much older man of her dreams. Her husband, a recent widower, was the owner of a prosperous ninety-acre farm near Westminster. To the outside world they looked like a well-to-do upper-class couple, but behind closed doors things weren't all that they seemed.

Thomas Cook was a man of many contrasts. He was disliked by most of his neighbors, who thought he had questionable morality. Most agreed that he was a shrewd businessman with keen financial abilities. It was universally agreed that he was cantankerous and quarrelsome in disposition. Very little is known about Katie Pope's early life other than she was born in 1872 in Westminster and raised on her parents' farm, neighbors of Thomas Cook.

In the early morning hours of August 28, 1899, Katie Cook shot and killed her husband as he slept at their Westminster farm. His sinful ways apparently caught up with him. In the years leading up to his death, he was involved in two shooting incidents, one in 1897 with his brother and another in October 1898, which resulted in the death of local farmer John Griggsby, who had accused Cook of insulting his wife. Cook was acquitted by reason of self-defense in the latter incident.

In the years preceding the tragedy, Katie had allegedly endured verbal

Modern-day photo of the old Orange County Courthouse, Santa Ana, California.

abuse and numerous degradations that included the flagrant infidelity of her husband. For ten nights prior to the shooting, her husband had snuck off to the bedroom of his lover, Mabel Moody, a young servant girl. Well aware of her husband's blatant unfaithfulness, Katie decided it was time to end the torment. When her husband returned to their bedroom around 3:00 a.m. and fell asleep, Katie silently retrieved a revolver from underneath her pillow. Standing directly over her sleeping husband, she pointed the revolver at his forehead and pulled the trigger, killing him instantly. Hearing the shot, Mabel Moody and ranch hand Jim Barton rushed into the room. Katie angrily confronted Moody, accusing her of causing the tragedy. Barton disarmed Katie and then called the county sheriff.

On October 10, Katie Cook was arraigned for murder and ordered to stand trial. She was the first woman charged with murder in Orange County history. Her murder trial began on December 18, before Judge Wesley Ballard. The prosecution declared that Katie was rational and sane when she shot and killed her husband and that the true motive for the killing wasn't jealousy of her husband's lover but monetary. Apparently when Thomas Cook was incarcerated for the shooting of John Griggsby, he had deeded his entire property to his wife as a gift to qualify her as a bondsman. After his discharge, a new deed transferring the property back to him was drawn up, signed, witnessed, and delivered to Cook by his wife, but the document was never recorded with the county. The prosecution alleged that, aside from being jealous about her husband, Katie wanted him out of the way in order to inherit his entire property, particularly as she knew that the deed she had given him—if indeed she ever gave one—had never been recorded.

The defendant was represented by prominent attorneys Victor Montgomery and Le Comte Davis, who alleged that their client had been wrought by mental anguish due to threats and the indiscretions of her husband prior to the shooting. This ill treatment rendered her mentally incompetent and innocent of her actions. The defense called more than two dozen witnesses to attest to the deceased's immoral reputation. One young girl testified that she and Katie were forced by threat of bodily harm to listen as Thomas Cook read pages of vulgar poetry. The defense also called four physicians to testify that the defendant was insane at the time of the shooting.

When Katie Cook began testifying on December 22, she recalled very little from the actual shooting but was able to describe in great detail the years of verbal abuse, orgies, and the numerous illicit affairs of her deceased husband. She tearfully testified that even though she had suffered greatly during their marriage, she still loved him but knew that his heart had turned away from her many years prior to the shooting. She stated that in the days leading up to the shooting, her husband had begun sleeping elsewhere, making the excuse that it was cooler in other rooms of the house. But she admitted that she knew this was just a ruse to conceal his true intentions of rendezvousing with his lover, Mabel Moody. She recounted how, night after night, she lay awake heartbroken as her husband snuck off. On the night of the shooting, she testified that a frenzy overcame her, and she lost control of her senses but had no further recollection of what happened.

On December 23, after five days of testimony, the jury of twelve men deliberated for only eighteen minutes before returning a verdict of not guilty. In the eyes of the jurors, Katie Cook had been justified in shooting her husband, who they viewed as being immoral and deserving of death. Upon hearing the verdict, the courtroom burst into applause. A visibly relieved Katie Cook was led from the courtroom by relatives and friends. After the trial, she returned to the farm to find comfort in the arms of loyal ranch hand Jim Barton, who had been employed at the ranch only two and a half months prior to the shooting tragedy. On April 17, 1900, they were secretly married in Riverside. The speed at which she had remarried and the amount of influence her new husband wielded raised concerns in the community, and people began to wonder what had really happened.

In the years following the trial, several lawsuits were filed against Katie and the estate of Thomas Cook, including one brought by the deceased's mother, Elizabeth Phillips. Since Cook had died without a proper will and had no children, half of the property was legally supposed to pass to Mrs. Phillips, but this was contested. The case was eventually settled, and the amount Mrs. Phillips received is not known. During these proceedings, there were allegations (which were never proven) that Katie wasn't the actual shooter and that Jim Barton might have played a more sinister role in the tragedy. During this same time, Katie also confided in a friend, Delia Rawson, that she wasn't really positive her husband was having an affair with Mabel Moody at the time of the shooting, which was in direct conflict with her sworn testimony during the trial and thus placed a giant shadow upon her acquittal. In 1901, Katie Cook-Barton filed a lawsuit against Rawson for defrauding her of some of her property, which was later decided in the plaintiff's favor.

In 1906, Jim Barton died and was buried just a few yards away from Thomas Cook at Santa Ana Cemetery, both graves unmarked. After the conclusion of the civil lawsuits and the death of her second husband, Katie Cook-Barton faded into the pages of California crime history, and no further information was found about her activities or whereabouts. To this day historians still speculate whether Katie actually pulled the trigger that fateful night in 1899. Whether her true motivation for shooting her husband was to escape an abusive relationship or other darker reasons will never be known for certain.

CHAPTER TWO

Dastardly Deeds in the Early Decades of the Twentieth Century

(1900-1919)

"After all, crime is only a left-handed form of human endeavor."

—John Huston (1906-1987)
Academy Award-winning director, screenwriter, actor

Old West Justice
CLARA WELLMAN
(1901, Riverside County)

Marriages: Some are long and some are short, but they're always filled with promise at the start. "For richer or poorer, in sickness and in health" are traditionally part of the vows. Those words are a contract that binds a couple together. But what if those binds become too tight? What then? Well, there's one way of loosening them, and it's found right there in those wedding vows . . . "Till death do us part."

As the twentieth century dawned in California, another young woman, much like Katie Cook, found herself trapped in an emotionally and physically abusive marriage that would ultimately lead to the death of the tormenting husband. Frank Pingrey Wellman was born on May 7, 1858, in Iowa, and moved to the Inland Empire area of southern California around 1885. He purchased a large cattle ranch in the San Jacinto Mountains near present-day Idyllwild. Wellman was considered a decent fellow by most, but when he drank he quickly turned mean and combative. He often threatened physical violence, especially to his neighbors and family. Newspaper accounts of the period tell of Wellman's exploits of terrorizing area ranchers by riding by their homes and firing his revolver indiscriminately and without warning.

Wellman was also alleged to have once been a confidant and companion of Old West desperado and convicted double murderer Charles Marshall, who shot and killed Deputy Sheriff Frank Hamilton and Albert Larsen in cold-blood in a saloon fight near San Jacinto, on April 9, 1895. Marshall was convicted of the double homicide and eventually hanged at San Quentin.

In the summer of 1895, Frank Wellman, thirty-six, met and married a thirteen-year-old girl named Clara Arnaiz, and together they would have two children. By the time Clara was nineteen she had already endured six years of emotional and physical abuse from her husband and desperately wanted out of their marriage. Frank refused a separation and allegedly threatened to kill her and their children if she ever tried to leave. Things became worse after the birth of their second child in March 1901. Wellman claimed the boy was not his and took out his anger on Clara and the child.

Things came to a boiling point on Sunday morning, August 4, 1901, when Wellman—in the throes of a weekend drinking binge—became irate when his infant son would not stop crying. He started yelling at Clara and began choking the baby. He also threatened to kill the whole family and take his own life. Fearing for the safety of her children and herself, Clara ran to a back bedroom and retrieved a loaded .22 caliber rifle. When her husband pulled a knife from his pocket, she pointed the gun at him and fired one shot. Wellman fell without uttering another word and died instantly.

The Riverside sheriff was summoned to the scene, and two days later a coroner's inquest was held. After brief testimony from Clara and several other witnesses, the jury found that she had acted in self-defense and that the killing of Frank Wellman was justified. She was exonerated of all blame in view of her husband's past character. When Wellman's father, Elijah, was informed of his son's death, he stated, "He that lives by the gun, dies by the gun. It was what I always expected for the past twenty years. He was always ready to pull his gun."

The case of Clara Wellman and others like it reflected the long-standing desire to protect women from enemy deviants, even when these women were bound to their assailant. The law, armed with Victorian values, often affirmed the rights of these women with verdicts of justifiable homicide when a male threatened to destroy the family. In October of 1902, Clara Wellman married another local cattle rancher, Joseph Hamilton, and they would have four children together.

According to newspapers of the time period, Frank Wellman was buried at San Jacinto Cemetery, but a search of cemetery records was unsuccessful in corroborating this information. Two well-known hiking trails are named after the ill-tempered and unfortunate rancher: Wellman Cieniga and Wellman's Divide. Both are accessed from the San Jacinto aerial tramway in Palm Springs. Clara Wellman-Hamilton's whereabouts after the death of her second husband in 1927 are not known.

The Trunk Murderess
EMMA LEDOUX
(1906, Stockton)

Stories about young, beautiful women accused of murdering someone they claimed to love will always capture the attention of the public and press. Two months after the Great San Francisco Earthquake of April 18, 1906, Emma Cole LeDoux was found guilty of murdering her third husband and stuffing his possibly not-quite-dead body in a trunk. The newspapers of the day devoted their front pages to her every movement, and she was dubbed "The Trunk Murderess." She has been erroneously credited as being the first woman in California to be sentenced to death, but, as we've learned earlier, that dubious distinction went to Laura Fair in 1871.

Emma LeDoux was born on September 10, 1872, in California, and from the start was a woman who did not play by Victorian society's unbending rules. She left husbands she didn't love, allegedly worked in San Francisco's brothels, and was stoic in the face of public hostility. Emma's free-thinking ways helped ambitious prosecutors convince a jury of her guilt, even though the case against her was based primarily on circumstantial evidence.

On the afternoon of March 24, 1906, the body of thirty-three-year-old Albert Newton McVicar was found stuffed in a trunk at the Southern Pacific Railroad Station in Stockton, California. He had been employed as a timberman in the Rawhide Mine in Tuolumne County and was estranged from his wife Emma LeDoux. Police immediately suspected her in his death when it was determined that she had purchased and arranged for the trunk's shipment. She was taken into custody two days later and returned to Stockton to stand trial.

Under interrogation, she confessed to knowing about the murder but denied having been the principal in it, initially naming Joe Miller, a friend of her husband, as the actual killer. She stated that on the night of Saturday, March 23, she, McVicar, and Miller had been drinking together at the California Hotel in Stockton. She recalled that around 12:30 a.m. a heated argument ensued between Miller and her husband, and she briefly left the room. When she returned she found her husband lying on the bed in a pool of vomit, apparently dead. Miller told her that McVicar had swallowed a bottle of carbonic acid.

In an excited state of mind, she asked Miller what they should do, and after further discussion Miller instructed her to buy a trunk and some rope, put the body in it, and send it to San Francisco to store it there for a year. That morning she did as Miller instructed, going to a local store to purchase the trunk and having it delivered to the hotel. Miller then directed LeDoux to say nothing or he'd kill her. She admitted to helping stuff the body into the trunk and accompanied it to the Stockton train depot. When the baggage master made comments about the unusual weight of the trunk and that a foul smell was emanating from it, LeDoux became nervous, abandoned the trunk, and took a train to San Francisco. She and Miller traveled together as far as Point Richmond, where he departed and she continued on to Antioch, where she was eventually taken into custody at the Arlington Hotel.

During the course of the investigation, police detectives uncovered that Emma had been married four times and that one of her husbands, William Williams, had died in Arizona in 1902 under suspicious circumstances. She married McVicar later that same year in Bisbee, Arizona, but they soon separated, and she returned to her mother's home in Amador County, California. In August 1905, she married Eugene LeDoux but never sought a divorce from McVicar.

Trunk in which Emma LeDoux placed the body of Albert McVicar is on display at the Haggin Museum in Stockton, California.

An autopsy of McVicar's body and other examinations of the remains came to differing conclusions regarding the cause of death. One expert determined that he had been beaten to death, while others stated he had been poisoned with chloral hydrate, commonly referred to as "knock-out drops." Later tests revealed that a lethal combination of morphine and chloral hydrate had caused the victim's death. Police investigators later determined that LeDoux had also purchased cyanide from a local pharmacy, but toxicology tests failed to show any sign of this drug in the victim's system. The coroner's jury concluded that McVicar's death was caused by a combination of a drug overdose of morphine and choral hydrate and injuries sustained when the victim's body was stuffed into the trunk. It was also determined that McVicar was still alive when he was placed in the trunk and that lack of oxygen also contributed to his demise. Emma LeDoux was named the perpetrator.

Prior to her trial, LeDoux revised her original statement to police, reversing her claim that Joe Miller was the killer, explaining that she was confused and had not seen her attorney prior to making the statement. She went on to name another man, Joe Healy—with whom she at one time had been engaged to marry—as the murderer. Police determined that Healy had an airtight alibi and was not present at the murder scene. Emma LeDoux was to stand trial on her own.

Prison booking photo of Emma LeDoux.

Criminal proceedings against LeDoux progressed slowly, but the trial finally began on June 5, 1906, before Superior Court Judge William B. Nutter. The prosecution's case centered on the bigamous relationship between Eugene LeDoux and the defendant and the fear of its exposure as the motivating factor in the death of McVicar. The defense claimed that the prosecution did not provide any direct evidence that LeDoux had poisoned McVicar and she could not be placed at the scene of the death. LeDoux refused to take the stand in her own defense and remained calm and composed throughout the entire proceedings. Her attorneys argued that McVicar had committed suicide by voluntarily ingesting a lethal concoction of drugs, and that he had placed himself inside the trunk.

On June 23, after three-plus weeks of contemptuous and sensational testimony, the all-male jury found LeDoux guilty of first-degree murder. As the verdict was read, the defendant showed little emotion and remained calm. Asked by reporters if she cared to make a statement, she politely declined and was taken from the courtroom.

On August 10, Judge Nutter sentenced her to death. "And it is the judgment of the court that you be hanged by the neck until you are dead. The court now issues the death warrant and fixes the time for the execution upon Friday October 19, 1906, between the hours of six o'clock in the morning and noon at the state prison at San Quentin." With a flushed face and heaving breasts, LeDoux listened as the sentence was read. She remained the same self-possessed women that she was throughout the trial.

After the sentence was pronounced, LeDoux rose from her chair and was led from the courtroom by sheriff's deputies. At the rear of the courtroom she was met by her mother, Mrs. Mary Head. As soon as she caught sight of her mother, Emma broke into a smile and they embraced warmly.

LeDoux's attorneys petitioned for a new trial and appealed the conviction. On May 19, 1909, LeDoux's murder conviction was overturned by the California Supreme Court on the grounds of procedural errors and juror prejudice. A new trial was set to begin on February 2, 1910, but on January 26, to avoid the death penalty, she pleaded guilty and was sentenced to life in prison. Ten years later, she was paroled.

Unrepentant for her crime, she eventually found herself back in jail after committing various parole violations. Over the next twenty years of her life, she remained in jail and was continually denied parole. She died from an undisclosed illness at a California women's detention facility on July 6, 1941, and was buried in an unmarked grave at the Union Cemetery in Bakersfield, California.

Murder, He Wrote
AURELIA SCHECK
(1906, Los Angeles)

Nineteen-year-old Aurelia Scheck, a young married woman who worked as a boardinghouse maid, felt trapped in a loveless marriage. Ernest Gary Stackpole was a carpenter with a criminal background who rented a room at Scheck's mother's boardinghouse in Los Angeles. Together, Aurelia and her lover plotted to murder her husband. During their short affair, Stackpole wrote dozens of love letters to his paramour in which he implicated himself as the mastermind behind the killing. These letters would later prove crucial in the case against him. But was Aurelia as naïve as she would later be portrayed? Or was she a coldhearted and calculating murderess?

Aurelia Scheck was born in 1887 in Iowa. Her parents separated when she was an infant, after which she and her mother traveled throughout the Midwest before finally settling in Los Angeles. She met her future husband, twenty-three-year-old Joel Scheck, while they both worked at a Los Angeles-area laundry. They were married in 1904, moved into a ramshackle apartment on San Julian Street, and struggled financially to make ends meet.

In early 1906, she met Ernest Stackpole, and they became close friends. At first the relationship was platonic, but he showered her with compliments and gifts. Because she was starved for attention and craved a financially secure life, the relationship soon became physically intimate. Their conversations turned to marriage and how to rid themselves of her husband.

In the early morning hours of June 14, 1906, an intruder broke into the Schecks's apartment. Joel Scheck was shot twice, in the chest and head, as he slept in his bed. Aurelia Scheck, who was unharmed in the attack, initially told police detectives that two burglars were responsible for the crime and that her husband had been shot when he woke up and surprised the intruders. Detectives were immediately suspicious of her story because there was little worth stealing in the dilapidated home, and nothing appeared to be out of place or missing. When Aurelia was taken to police headquarters the next day, her story began to unravel, and she confessed that she and her lover, Ernest Stackpole, had conspired to kill her husband and collect a $500 life insurance policy.

Both Scheck and Stackpole were held in custody while circumstantial evidence such as a bloody coat was discovered in Stackpole's rented room. Witnesses and family members of the accused were questioned. Aurelia was allowed to leave jail to attend the funeral of her husband at Evergreen Cemetery on Sunday, June 17, but showed very little emotion and refused to leave her carriage. Three days later, Stackpole and Scheck were charged with first-degree murder, but Aurelia was too ill to attend the arraignment hearing. In order to avoid prison time and in exchange for immunity, she struck a deal with prosecutors and agreed to testify against Stackpole. She remained at the county jail pending the conclusion of the proceedings.

Ernest Stackpole's murder trial began on August 7, and the prosecution's star witness, Aurelia Scheck took the stand and testified that she and the defendant had been having an affair for several months prior to the killing of her husband. She recalled that on the morning of June 13, she and Stackpole had met to discuss how they would murder her husband, and it was the defendant who came up with the idea to shoot him and pin the murder on burglars. She told the court that on the night of the murder, she had a late dinner with her husband, and they went to bed. She recalled lying awake, anxiously waiting for her lover to return. Several hours passed until she was startled by a noise from the back of the house. She arose to find Stackpole in the kitchen, wearing a mask and holding a revolver. Without saying a word, he pushed past her and fired two gunshots. Stackpole emerged from the bedroom and said, "Give me ten or fifteen minutes to get back to my room and then yell for help and tell of the burglars." He then left, and Aurelia went into the bedroom, where she found her husband dead in a pool of blood on their bed. A few minutes later, she went to neighbors for help. After she concluded her testimony, there were several more days of expert witness testimony before the prosecution rested its case.

To counter Aurelia Scheck's damning testimony, the defense attempted to discredit her character and reliability. They described her as a liar who often fabricated stories. They also tried to convince the jury that the victim might have committed suicide, although several expert witnesses refuted this claim as being highly unlikely. Stackpole took the stand briefly in his own defense, asserting his innocence and alleging a flimsy alibi that he had been with friends, watching a neighborhood fire on the night of the killing. None of his statements were corroborated.

On August 19, after nearly two weeks of testimony and twenty-eight hours of deliberation, the jury found Stackpole guilty of first-degree murder, and he was sentenced to life in prison. When the sentence was read, the defendant's head drooped forward, and he began to sob convulsively. As he was led away, a chorus of young children were heard from a nearby detention home, their haunting melody echoing throughout the courtroom: "Trust and obey, for there's no other way, to be happy in Jesus, but to trust and obey." Although Aurelia Scheck escaped murder charges in exchange for her testimony, the district attorney decided to press forward with perjury charges. She remained in jail for another three months before those charges were dropped, and she was released from custody. Following her release, she disappeared from the headlines, and nothing further is known.

As for Stackpole, he remained at the county jail pending appeal of his conviction. On April 4, 1907, he and two fellow inmates attempted to escape. Armed with lead pipes, the three men tried to overpower two guards. The attack was thwarted when one of the guards drew his revolver and shot two of the attackers. Stackpole was uninjured and surrendered when additional guards arrived on the scene. The next day, Stackpole was sent north to San Quentin, where he was denied a new trial and spent the remainder of his life in prison.

The Red Murderess
DORA CHIPP
(1906, Humboldt County)

Willow Creek is a rugged mountain community nestled in the heart of the Six Rivers National Forest area of Northern California, near the Oregon border. The first non-indigenous settlers to inhabit the area were Chinese laborers arriving from the mining and lumber camps in the mid-1870s, which earned the town the name China Flat. In the summer of 1906, the sparsely inhabited community was rocked by a horrific murder with racial undertones that found its way to the front pages of newspapers throughout the state of California.

On the afternoon of June 17, 1906, Mrs. William Beale of Willow Creek, California—the young wife of a well-known local rancher—and her two young children were riding in a carriage on a country road near their home when they were assaulted by Dora Chipp. The attacker, a local woman of Native American descent, allegedly held a long-standing grudge against the Beales and wanted to start some trouble. Grasping the reins of Mrs. Beale's horse and menacingly waving a loaded revolver, Chipp brought the carriage to a halt. Threats and racial insults were hurled between the two women before Beale sprang from her carriage to protect her children. She was able to knock Chipp from her horse as the two women engaged in a fierce struggle for the revolver. In the brawl, the weapon discharged several times with one shot lightly grazing Beale's chin.

In mortal fear for her life, Beale broke free from her attacker and ran to a home owned by Ida Seaver. As Beale ran away, she could hear several more gunshots. Chipp then remounted her horse and fled the scene. It was soon discovered that Beale's seventeen-month-old daughter, Silvia, had been shot twice in the head and was lying motionless on the side of the road near the carriage. Beale's older child, five-year-old Gladys, was able to flee on foot and was unharmed.

On the early afternoon of June 19, two days after the shooting, a sheriff's posse apprehended Chipp without incident near the town of Bonanza in Klamath County, Oregon. She was riding horseback and speeding north toward the Yainax Indian Reservation, where she hoped to gain sanctuary. Chipp was arrested with a .22 caliber rifle. She was transported back to Willow Creek and charged with first-degree murder.

Because of the racial undertones of the case and the threat of lynching, the trial was postponed and moved north to Yreka, the county seat of Siskiyou County. Newspapers across California sent reporters to cover the trial, and headlines dubbed her the "The Red Murderess." The proceedings began on August 21 before Superior Court Judge James S. Beard. Several prominent Indian tribes helped contribute to her defense fund and strongly protested the death penalty under threat of violence. This caused a tense standoff between local law enforcement and tribal leaders.

Prosecutors did not bow to pressure from these outside forces and continued to seek execution of the defendant. They began their case by showing that Chipp had a long history of violent behavior and had premeditated the attack on Mrs. Beale. They showed that bad blood had simmered between the defendant and the Beales for several months prior to the tragedy, caused by a horse trade that had gone wrong. Because of this, Chipp felt insulted and sought revenge against the Beales. Several witnesses, including the defendant's own sister, testified that Chipp had stalked Beale for a number of days prior to the altercation.

On August 25, the defendant took the stand in her own defense and agreed that there had been difficulties between herself and the Beales but denied planning the altercation that led to the death of Silvia Beale. She insisted that they had met on the road by accident and that Mrs. Beale was the initial aggressor. Chipp testified that Mrs. Beale began calling her derogatory names and struck her horse with a whip. She went on to state that she was carrying a loaded rifle on the day of the altercation but had no intention of using it and denied threatening the victims. Continuing her testimony, Chipp went on to state that during the fight with Beale her revolver somehow fell from her pocket and discharged accidentally, striking the young child. Asked why she had fled the scene, the defendant said she feared she'd be lynched on the spot if caught by the local ranchers. After her testimony, the defense rested its case.

The following day, after five days of testimony and several hours of deliberation, the all-white male jury agreed that the prosecution's case was lacking and found the defendant guilty of the lesser charge of second-degree murder. Several ballots were held before the jurors agreed on a compromise verdict. The maximum penalty was life imprisonment, but it was anticipated the sentence would be much less. On September 15, Chipp was sentenced to twenty years imprisonment at San Quentin. Judge Beard commented that in his forty years of experience, every criminal who was sentenced to life had been pardoned sooner or later. What became of Chipp after her conviction and incarceration and whether or not she was ever released from custody is not known.

Killing on Principle
ANGELA DE VITA
(1906, Los Angeles)

On November 21, 1910, Angela Maria De Vita—a thirty-five-year-old happily married woman with four young children—shot and killed Abele Bevo on the streets of Los Angeles. Bevo, an Italian immigrant, was a former lodger at the De Vita home. He was infatuated with De Vita and attempted, over a two-month period, to persuade her to leave her husband. Undeterred by her refusals, Bevo became more agitated and aggressive, going as far as to threaten to blow up her home and kill her family if she continued to refuse his advances.

On the morning of the shooting, after leaving the house of a friend on Alpine Street, De Vita was confronted by Bevo, who was standing at the gate of the home. She tried to avoid him, but he insisted on walking with her. Along the way, a very animated Bevo again tried to persuade De Vita to leave her husband. After walking a short distance, De Vita tired of Bevo's pestering and hailed a cable car. Undeterred, Bevo also got on and continued his harassment. They rode together as far as Main and Lamar Streets, where De Vita attempted to exit the cable car. Bevo, agitated by her attempt to flee, grabbed her wrist in a vain attempt to keep her on board. Fearing for her life, De Vita pulled a small .38 caliber revolver from beneath her shawl and shot him five times in the chest, killing him instantly. A nearby police officer heard the shots and rushed to the scene. De Vita was standing over Bevo crying: "I'm glad I did it. He deserved what I've given him." She was taken into custody without further resistance and charged with murder.

De Vita's ill-advised trial began on February 20, 1911, with the prosecution presenting very little evidence. De Vita took the stand in her own defense and testified that she loved her family and husband, and she detailed the months of terror and intimidation she had suffered at the hands of the deceased. Her testimony was so convincing that the prosecution refused to cross-examine her on the strength of her statements. After two days of proceedings, the jury took three minutes of deliberation to find De Vita not guilty, believing she had acted in self-defense. The shooting of Abele Bevo was determined to be justifiable homicide.

A Woman's Desperation
LEA DELMON
(1913, Los Angeles)

On the evening of July 27, 1913, twenty-three-year-old Lea Delmon shot and killed her husband as he slept at their ramshackle apartment near the old plaza center of Los Angeles. Police were summoned to the scene by neighbors and found Delmon sobbing over the dead man's body. He had been shot once in the head. A distraught Lea told detectives that she had felt compelled to shoot and kill him after suffering years of emotional and physical abuse that included forced prostitution. She was arrested and taken into custody and held at the city jail pending a coroner's inquest.

Lea Delmon was born in Belgium in 1890; at the age of sixteen, she came to San Francisco with her mother. On April 18, 1906, her mother was killed in the Great Earthquake, and several days after the disaster, Lea met Louis Delmon, who promised to protect and shelter her. Almost immediately he became physically abusive and forced her into prostitution. In 1908, they moved to Salt Lake City, and after much coaxing by Lea, they were married. For a brief period, they tried to live a righteous lifestyle and appeared to be happy, but Louis soon returned to his hedonistic lifestyle. The couple moved to Los Angeles in the spring of 1913, and Lea was again forced into immoral

Character sketch of Lea Delmon at the Coroner's inquest held on July 28, 1913. *Courtesy of the* Los Angeles Times.

activities. The physical abuse intensified, and on the morning of the shooting, she sustained one last beating, which pushed her over the edge. She decided it was time to end her torment once and for all. That evening, after Louis had fallen asleep, Lea took a loaded revolver from the nightstand, silently crept to her husband's bedside, pointed the weapon point blank at the side of his head, and pulled the trigger, killing him instantly.

On July 29, a coroner's inquest was held at the Button mortuary, and hundreds of curious onlookers attempted to gain access to the proceedings. During several hours of testimony, Lea Delmon recalled the years of emotional and physical abuse she suffered at the hands of her husband. She also detailed the years of forced prostitution that led to the shooting. She testified that even though she had suffered these tremendous indignities, she still loved him. The jury deliberated for only a few minutes and returned a verdict of justifiable homicide. The jury foreman stated: "The wife who shoots her husband when he would force her into a life of shame commits a justifiable homicide." The Los Angeles district attorney refused to press the case any further, stating: "The State takes no attitude of revenge or reparation. It is possible the slain man had forfeited all consideration, even perhaps the right to live." Delmon was released from custody.

But this was not the end of Lea Delmon's legal troubles. Her sister-in-law, Louise Pons of San Jose, contested the estate of her deceased brother. Pons's point of contention was Lea's integrity and competency to handle the estate and the fact that she had allegedly premeditated the killing of her husband in order to acquire her husband's assets. The civil proceedings began on October 11, and Delmon was once again forced to recall the years of abuse and forced sexual degradation at the hands of her husband. After four days of contentious testimony, the jury determined that Delmon had the full right to administer and collect her deceased husband's $8,000 estate. After the conclusion of the proceedings, Delmon used this money to purchase the Plaza Boarding House on North Main Street and faded from the headlines.

The Money Maniac

ANNA HAMMOND

(1917, Fresno County)

O n April 16, 1917, law enforcement officials discovered the body of wealthy Fresno County farmer Faustin Lassere buried in a shallow grave near a barn on his ranch. He had been missing for several weeks. The following day, thirty-year-old Charles Hammond and his twenty-six-year-old wife, Anna, were arrested and charged with his murder.

The Hammonds confessed to police that they had committed bigamy and that they plotted to carry out the brutal murder to gain the victim's wealth and property. They admitted to burying the victim's body in a shallow grave and spending his money until they were discovered. Both accused each other of being the mastermind behind the plot. Charles claimed his wife was a "money maniac" and had become a modern-day vampire, plotting similar crimes throughout the county. Meanwhile, Anna told detectives that Charles was the instigator behind the crime and that he had forced her to marry Lassere.

In February 1917, Faustin Lassere, forty-seven, had married Anna Hammond using the name Lillie Harper in Madera, California, following a brief engagement. She had answered his advertisement in a local newspaper for a housekeeper. Several days after the nuptials, Charles Hammond arrived at the farm pretending to be a laborer in need of work. A naïve Lassere believed his story, and for the next few weeks all three lived together on the farm without incident.

On the evening of March 30, the Hammonds carried out their foul plot, and Lassere was murdered as he sat having dinner. On the pretext of getting something from a kitchen cabinet, Anna retrieved a hammer and repeatedly struck her unsuspecting husband on the back of his head. The blows were not fatal, and Charles was forced to shoot him six times and slit his throat with a knife for good measure. Together they buried Lassere's body in a shallow grave behind a barn on the property. Following the slaying, they continued to live on the property, spending the victim's money. On April 16, after they attempted to forge the deed to Lassere's farm, suspicious bank officials notified law enforcement.

The Hammonds' trial began with jury selection on June 5, and the following day prosecutors announced that the defendants had agreed to plead guilty to avoid the death penalty. On June 7, they were formally sentenced to life in prison. On October 5, 1926, Charles Hammond escaped from

Folsom Prison, East Gate. *Courtesy of Publicdomainpictures.net.*

Folsom Prison while working at the penitentiary's honor farm and for the next seven years remained a fugitive from justice. He assumed an alias, Carl M. Hammond, married, and began operating a berry and chicken farm in Fresno. On October 28, 1933, law enforcement officials were tipped off to his whereabouts, and he was taken into custody at his home without incident. When Hammond's new wife was informed of her husband's true identity, she was dumbfounded and stated that she never suspected anything about his notorious past. No further information was uncovered regarding Charles Hammond's remaining time in prison or whether he was ever granted parole.

In 1935, Anna Hammond was released on parole and relocated to Washington. Four years later she violated terms of her release and was returned to California to serve out her sentence. In the coming years, she unsuccessfully petitioned the governor's office for clemency. In 1943, she was again released from custody and the following year obtained a formal divorce from Charles on the grounds of cruelty. What happened to her following her release is not known.

Murder or Suicide?

GERTRUDE GIBBONS

(1918, Los Angeles)

On the afternoon of December 15, 1918, Pullman train conductor Frank G. Gibbons, thirty-eight, was suddenly taken ill and collapsed at the Santa Fe train depot in downtown Los Angeles. He was rushed to his home on South Bonnie Brae Avenue in an unconscious state and died a few hours later without regaining consciousness. The first indication that his sudden and mysterious death might not have been from natural causes came the following day when several coworkers told police they suspected foul play. Law enforcement authorities then opened a full inquiry into the death.

Police investigators soon discovered that Frank's forty-five-year-old wife, Gertrude, had recently purchased a packet of cyanide from a local drugstore. When confronted with these facts, she confessed that she had bought the drugs at her husband's request and had given him the poison so he could commit suicide. In further statements she detailed years of jealousy and unhappiness in their marriage. They had moved to Los Angeles from Boston in early 1914, because he suffered from tuberculosis, and they thought the climate change might help his condition. They were married on February

The Santa Fe Train Depot in Los Angeles, undated photograph. *Courtesy of the* Los Angeles Times.

3 of that same year. Gradually his health began to fail, and Frank allegedly implored his wife to help him end his suffering. She finally relented and agreed to help. On Friday, December 13, she went to Nelson's Drugstore at the corner of Sixth and Hill Streets and, using a false name, secured a packet of cyanide of potassium. When she returned home, she gave her husband the drug, and for the next several days she lived in a constant state of fear, knowing that one day he would be dead. She also told police that she didn't initially divulge this information to doctors because she feared the consequences of her acts.

Police were skeptical of Gertrude's statements and believed that she had intentionally substituted the deadly poison for his regular medicine. Coworkers of the deceased stated that on the day of Gibbons's death, he appeared to be in good spirits and made every effort to perform his regular work duties. Police used these statements to prove that Frank Gibbons had not intended to kill himself and that he had swallowed the poison believing he was taking regular medications. On December 18, a warrant was issued for Gertrude Gibbons's arrest, and she was taken into custody and charged with first-degree murder. The motive for the crime was alleged to have been a life-insurance policy worth around $3,200 and the desire to rid herself of an invalid husband.

Two days later, in a twist of fate, the official coroner's report disclosed that there were no traces of cyanide in Gibbons's system and that he had died from a pulmonary hemorrhage caused from the tuberculosis. Undaunted by the news, the district attorney requested another autopsy be performed and held Gertrude pending the results. When told of the results, she repeated her story that she had given her husband the poison at his own request. Under California law at the time, it was a felony to knowingly supply a person with the instruments for an attempt at suicide—an act that she freely admitted she had done.

As law enforcement awaited results of the second autopsy, attention soon turned to Gertrude's past. A newspaper reporter from the *Los Angeles Times* discovered that she had been married before and had apparently never obtained a divorce. Josiah Herrick, Gertrude's previous husband, told authorities that they had married in 1898, in Gloucester, Massachusetts, and after several years agreed to separate but never obtained an official divorce. Gertrude now faced the possibility of bigamy and murder charges.

In late December, the results of the second autopsy discovered trace elements of cyanide in the body of Frank Gibbons. As a result of these new findings, the case was remanded to the Los Angeles Grand Jury for review. On January 13, after several weeks of contemptuous testimony, the grand jury refused to indict Gertrude Gibbons on murder charges. Prosecutors dropped the charges, and she was freed from custody.

Upon her release, she made a statement to the press: "I am a different woman from the one who was brought here charged with murder. At first I did not know whether my husband had taken poison. I was always willing to help him, even at the risk of committing a crime in law, but not before God. I was devoted to his interest. While I have been in jail I have studied philosophy, with the idea of teaching it when I leave here. I want to teach people to be happy. I shall try to be forgotten by going somewhere where no one knows me." Since nothing else is known about her, apparently Gibbons was successful in her plans.

CHAPTER THREE

Notorious Crimes of the Roaring Twenties

(1920-1929)

"There is no development strategy more beneficial to society as a whole—women and men alike—than the one which involves women as central players."

—Kofi Annan
Former Secretary-General of the United Nations

A Contemptuous Paramour's Ultimate Demise

MARIE LEONARD BAILEY

(1920, Pasadena)

On the night of December 22, 1920, Marie Leonard Bailey—a twenty-one-year-old married woman and part-time stage actress—shot and killed her lover, twenty-four-year-old Clarence Hogan, on a secluded road in the foothills near Pasadena. The young wife of Canadian motion picture executive Edwin Bailey, Marie had been carrying on an affair with Hogan for several years and was estranged from her husband at the time of the shooting. The victim was from Oakland—he was a handsome and charismatic traveling salesman for a record company and a familiar figure around Los Angeles's entertainment industry. He was also an aspiring model and actor, who had appeared in several motion pictures in minor roles.

On the fateful night, Bailey and Hogan had taken a scenic drive in a vain attempt to work through some relationship issues. Bailey initially told detectives that she had planned to kill herself when it became clear Hogan had no intention of proposing marriage. When she pulled out a gun and informed Hogan of her suicide plans, he callously taunted her, stating, "Well, why don't you kill yourself then?" Enraged by his uncaring attitude, she pointed the gun at his chest and pulled the trigger. Hogan staggered from the car and fell dead on the side of the road. Bailey then exited the car and fired two more shots in the air before running hysterically from the scene. A short distance away, she flagged down a passing motorist, who then contacted police.

The next day a coroner's jury was convened in Pasadena and determined that Bailey had acted with intent to murder when she shot Hogan. She was charged with first-degree murder and held without bail. At her preliminary hearing on December 31, she stood silent and expressionless as the charges and events of the day were recounted in court. In the months leading up to her murder trial, Bailey's defense attorneys began to spin a different version of the case in the press. They described the defendant as being despondent after discovering that her lover was not the man she thought he was and because of this had resolved to commit suicide. They claimed that while the victim was trying to prevent her from harming herself, the gun had discharged accidentally.

Bailey's murder trial began on May 25, 1921, and over the next few days numerous witnesses were called to testify. The defendant took the stand in her own defense the following day and bared her soul regarding the details of her failed marriage and illicit affair with the victim. Her testimony focused primarily on the unintentional firing of the gun and her despondent and irrational state of mind at the time of the shooting. She stated that Hogan was having financial difficulties for which he blamed the defendant and had asked to borrow hundreds of dollars to fix an automobile. On the night of the shooting, they drove from her father's home in Altadena, and she recalled becoming paralyzed with emotion in the startling realization that her lover wasn't the man she thought he was and became acutely aware that there was no future in the relationship. By chance, she found her father's revolver stashed between the cushions of the car. She told Hogan that she no longer wished to live and pointed the weapon at herself. She recalled that Hogan's initial response was callous and taunting, but eventually he attempted to seize the gun from her, and that was when it discharged by accident, fatally striking him in the chest.

Following her dramatic full day of testimony, the defense and prosecution rested their cases, and the jury of nine women and three men began deliberations. It took them only five hours to render a verdict, and as they entered the courtroom their evasion of eye contact with the defendant foreshadowed an ominous outcome. As the guilty verdict of manslaughter, rather than first-degree murder was read, Bailey was racked with despair and wept openly. Her initial admissions to police and testimony by crime scene witnesses weighed heavily on the jury's lesser verdict, as did her age and the circumstances surrounding her failed marriage and tragic love affair with the victim.

Press coverage of the trial included frequent pictures of a very young, attractive woman. Perhaps it was those photographs, and more likely her age and circumstances that drew the sympathy of the jury and resulted in a conviction for a lesser offense. On June 1, Los Angeles County Superior Court Judge McCormick sentenced Bailey to serve a prison term at San Quentin from one to ten years.

In the end, the verdict showed that there had been intent to kill, but the lesser finding of manslaughter demonstrated that the shooting was not premeditated, and other circumstances allowed for clemency for the defendant. Details of Bailey's life behind bars and her whereabouts after her assumed release are not known.

The Black Widow
LOUISE PEETE
(1920-1947, Los Angeles)

ouise Peete was both refined and elegant, but she murdered for profit. She was a master manipulator of male weaknesses and excelled in feminine charms. A callous and calculating cold-blooded killer, she showed no sign of remorse for her crimes or victims. Her reign of terror lasted nearly four decades before she was apprehended. Incredibly, all four of her husbands would die suspiciously or from suicide. Peete would eventually pay the ultimate price for a lifetime of sin, deceit, and murder. She has been identified as one of America's first female serial killers and has the dubious distinction of being one of only four women ever executed in California's gas chamber.

She was born Lofie Louise Preslar on September 20, 1880, in Bienville, Louisiana, the daughter of a socially prominent New Orleans newspaper publisher. In her youth, Louise lived a life of privilege and attended the best private schools. While in school she gained a reputation for her sexual escapades and other inappropriate behaviors, for which she was eventually expelled, after which she then moved to Boston and began working as a high-class call girl.

In 1903, at the age of twenty-three, she married Henry Bosley, a traveling salesman. Three years later, during the summer of 1906, Henry caught his wife in bed with another man. Grief-stricken and heartbroken, Bosley committed suicide. After her husband's death, Louise sold all of her marital belongings and moved to Shreveport, Louisiana, where under financial strains she again resorted to a life of prostitution to pay her bills. The change of scenery meant little to Louise, who continued to use her wanton sexuality and talents of seduction to charm unsuspecting men out of their money. During her many clandestine rendezvous, she often stole valuables and sold the objects for profit. In time, these thefts were discovered and pressed with the threat of exposure and possible criminal charges; she decided to move to Waco, Texas.

In Texas, she continued to ply her unsavory trade and quickly won the affection of Joe Appel, a wealthy oilman, who was best known for wearing flashy diamond rings and gold belt buckles. One week after meeting Louise, Appel was found dead with a bullet in his head and his expensive jewelry missing. Called before a special grand jury, Louise tearfully admitted that she had shot Appel, explaining that she did it out of self-defense. She told the all-male jury that the deceased had become violent and had tried to rape her, and fearing for her life she felt compelled to defend herself with fatal results. The jury believed the attractive Southern belle's account of the shooting and openly applauded as they set her free. Appel's missing diamonds were never found.

By 1913, running out of luck and in need of more cash, Louise moved to Dallas, Texas, and became acquainted with and married a local hotel clerk named Harry Faurote. The marriage was primarily a relationship of convenience for Louise, who openly flaunted numerous affairs during the couple's two years of marriage. These illicit liaisons soon took their toll on a mentally distraught Faurote, who committed suicide by hanging himself when the sins of his wife's promiscuity became too much to bear.

Soon after Faurote's death, Louise moved again—this time to Denver, Colorado, where she met and won the heart of Richard Peete, a door-to-door salesman. The couple married and bought a tiny home. Louise became pregnant and gave birth to a baby daughter a year later. By 1920, Louise had tired of her trivial domestic lifestyle that did not measure up to her standard of living, and she abandoned the family for California.

In Los Angeles, while looking for a place to live, she met Jacob Charles Denton, forty-nine, a recently widowed wealthy mining executive. Quickly winning his affections, she agreed to live with him at his Wilshire Boulevard mansion under the pretext of serving as a live-in companion, lover, and housekeeper. After several weeks of torrid sex, Louise abruptly asked Denton to marry her, but he politely refused the offer. For Denton this rejection was a fatal error. Smiling through this hurtful rebuff and humiliation, Louise soon began planning her paramour's demise.

In late May 1920, Denton disappeared without a trace, and Louise explained away his unexpected absence as an urgent last-minute business trip. Several weeks later, Denton's business associates and neighbors began to question his whereabouts. Louise, always ready with an explanation, concocted wild stories to cover up her involvement in his disappearance. By September, Denton's attorneys grew impatient and demanded police search Denton's mansion. After an hour, police discovered Denton's body buried in a shallow grave in the basement. By this time, Louise had already fled Los Angeles for Denver, where she had resumed a life with her estranged husband, Richard Peete.

Charged with first-degree murder, Louise was arrested and brought back to Los Angeles. Her trial began on January 21, 1921, and because of the lurid details of the case that had been leaked to the press, the proceedings became circus-like, with thousands of people lining the streets of downtown Los Angeles in an attempt to catch a glimpse of Peete as she arrived at the criminal courts building.

From the outset, defense attorneys attempted to plant reasonable doubt into the minds of the jury by pressing the opinion that the defendant, being

Gravesite of Jacob Denton at Hollywood Forever Cemetery in Los Angeles.

Louise Peete testifying during her 1921 murder trial. *Courtesy of the Los Angeles Times photographic archives collection, University of California, Los Angeles.*

of slight stature, didn't have the physical strength to drag the victim's body into the basement and could not have possibly committed the crime. The prosecution successfully discredited every defense allegation with one witness after another. When Peete testified in her own defense, she proclaimed her innocence and continued to state that she had no idea who had killed Denton. On February 5, unmoved by Peete's testimony, and after deliberating for less than four hours, the all-male jury found her guilty of first-degree murder. As the verdict was being read, Peete showed no emotion and sat reading quietly. Two weeks later, Superior Court Judge Frank R. Willis formally sentenced Peete to life in prison, and she was sent to San Quentin to serve out her punishment.

During the early years of his estranged wife's incarceration, Richard Peete corresponded regularly with Louise, but absence did not make her heart grow fonder. In 1924, after numerous letters went unanswered, Richard committed suicide. It was reported that while in prison she liked to boast to other inmates about the lovers she had driven to their deaths, and she especially cherished Richard's suicide as proof that even prison walls could not contain her fatal charm. In 1939, after serving eighteen years in prison, Peete was granted parole and released from custody to the care of Jessie Marcy, a woman who had steadfastly lobbied for her release. The court granted Louise's request for a name change to avoid publicity. Now known as Anna Lee, Peete found employment as a housekeeper for several wealthy Los Angeles-area residents.

Three years later, Jessie Marcy was found dead from an apparent stroke, but her home had been ransacked. Having no place to live, Peete, under the alias of Anna Lee, moved in with her probation officer, Emily Latham. On September 14, 1943, Latham died from an apparent heart attack. In what can only be described as a careless and inept investigation, neither of these deaths were seriously probed by police, who were unaware that Anna Lee was notorious convicted murderess Louise Peete.

Again, having no place to live, Peete turned to Margaret and Arthur Logan—the couple that had helped raise her daughter, Elizabeth, while she was in prison. Louise agreed to help with housework in exchange for free room and board at the Logan's Pacific Palisades home. In May 1944, Peete married sixty-seven-year-old Lee Borden Judson, a former advertising executive, who was oblivious to the fact that he had just married a convicted murderess.

Later that same month, Margaret Logan mysteriously vanished without a trace. Immediately, a suspicious mound of fresh dirt, marked with an array of colorful flowerpots, was found in the Logan's garden. Louise told Margaret's elderly husband that his wife was in the hospital and unable to receive visitors. By late June, Louise had persuaded authorities that Arthur Logan was mentally unbalanced, and he was committed to the Patton state asylum, where he died on December 6, 1944. With the Logans now out of the way, Louise moved into their home with her new husband. In short order, Lee Judson discovered a bullet hole in one wall of the house, a mysterious mound of earth in the garden, and an insurance policy naming his new wife as Margaret Logan's sole beneficiary. Despite being aware that something sinister might have happened to Mrs. Logan, Judson shockingly said nothing and remained silent.

By December 1944, Louise's parole officer had also grown uncertain of the irregular reports of Margaret Logan's disappearance, and police were dispatched to the Logan home to look for clues to her whereabouts. These searches prompted Lee Judson to voice his suspicions, and Margaret Logan's body was soon discovered buried under an avocado tree in a shallow grave two feet from the house. When questioned about the discovery, Louise, in a feeble attempt to deflect blame for the crime, stated that Arthur Logan had shot and killed his wife in a fit of rage. Frightened that her criminal history might make her a suspect, she agreed to help bury Margaret's body in the garden and then had Arthur committed to the asylum. Police did not believe Louise's story, and she was arrested on December 20 and charged with Margaret Logan's murder. Lee Judson was also arrested and charged as an accessory to the crime. He vehemently denied any knowledge of the murder. On January 12, 1945, the charges were dismissed for lack of evidence, and the next day, Judson climbed to the ninth floor stairwell of the Spring Arcade Building in the city's financial district and leapt to his death. Louise Peete, when informed of her husband's suicide, wept hysterically and stated, "I'm to blame for that ... he couldn't take disgrace. As long as I'm associated with him he was a marked man."

Gravesite of Margaret and Arthur Logan at Mountain View Cemetery in Altadena, California.

Louise Peete on the witness stand during her 1945 murder trial. *Courtesy of the Los Angeles Times photographic archives collection, University of California, Los Angeles.*

Peete's second murder trial began on April 23, 1945, and the defense relied primarily on reasonable doubt, while the prosecution argued that Peete had killed Margaret Logan to gain control of her property and other finances. On May 28, after five weeks of scandalous testimony, Louise Peete's fate was handed to the jury. After only three hours of deliberations—faced with overriding physical evidence, clear motive, and opportunity to commit the crime—they were unanimous in their verdict of guilty of first-degree murder. As the verdict was read, Peete remained calm and emotionless. While awaiting the jury's decision, she read a copy of Lin Yutang's, *The Importance of Living.* After the verdict was rendered, Peete callously told reporters, "Halfway through the trial I was sure what it would be. It's too bad Mrs. Logan wasn't in the courtroom to see how unjust that verdict was."

On June 1, Superior Court Judge Harold B. Landreth sentenced Peete to death in San Quentin's gas chamber. As the sentence was read, the sixty-three-year-old twice-convicted murderess remained calm, showing very little emotion. On April 11, 1947, after numerous appeals and stays of execution, she was executed in San Quentin's gas chamber. She met her fate with composed resignation and showed no remorse for her crimes. When asked by the prison warden if she was ready, Peete allegedly remarked, "I've been ready for a long time." She was the second woman to die in California's gas chamber. After the execution, Peete's body was released to a friend and cremated. Her ashes were buried in an unmarked grave at Angelus-Rosedale Cemetery in Los Angeles.

San Quentin's warden, Clinton Duffy, once described Louise Peete as projecting "an air of innocent sweetness, which masked a heart of ice." She died one of California's most notorious killers with a procession of death and suicide following her that is unrivaled in the annals of American criminal history. Possessed with a cold and cunning charm and an uncanny ability to attract weak and feebleminded men, Peete learned early in life how to use her deadly talents to gain what she wanted.

A Matter of Life and Death
NETTIE PLATZ
(1921, Los Angeles County)

Acton, California, is a tiny community located in the Sierra Pelona Mountains, fifty miles north of downtown Los Angeles. It was founded in the late 1880s as a camp for laborers who were building the Southern Pacific Railroad. It was later known for its gold and copper mines and ranching industries. On a warm summer morning in 1921, the quiet and gentile nature of the community was shattered by the shooting death of a local rancher.

Sixteen-year-old Nettie Platz was the beautiful young wife of a prominent Acton rancher. On July 13, 1921, she shot and killed her brother-in-law, thirty-six-year-old Earnest Platz, at her home. Nettie told Los Angeles County Sheriff's deputies that two weeks prior to the shooting, her husband and Earnest had gotten into an argument over the latter's lazy work habits in the fields. The quarrel continued to escalate without any foreseeable resolution. On the day of the shooting, Nettie and Earnest were alone at the ranch house when he became agitated and argumentative. She refused to engage him, and he became even more furious. Out of nowhere, he grabbed Nettie and began punching, scratching, and biting her in an all-out attack. Hearing what he thought was his brother coming home, Earnest stopped the assault and retreated to his upstairs bedroom. Fearing for her life and believing the attack might continue at any moment, Nettie retrieved a shotgun from a closet and followed Earnest upstairs. She found him lying on a bed in his room. When he lunged at her, Nettie leveled the weapon and pulled the trigger, hitting him in the chest and head, killing him instantly.

Nettie was taken into custody and brought to Los Angeles pending a coroner's jury and the district attorney's review of the case. A coroner's jury was convened two days later. Nettie's husband testified that he had recently been in a verbal confrontation with his brother. The argument was related to work criticism, and allegedly the deceased had threatened to do harm to the family. He also testified that his brother had a long history of mental illness and violence and that he had instructed his wife to kill Earnest if she was ever attacked. Nettie also testified and showed the jury the bruising and bite marks she had sustained in the vicious attack. The simple act of self-defense was enough for the jury, who deliberated for only three minutes before returning a verdict of justifiable homicide. The district attorney refused to press any further action in the case, and Nettie Platz was released from custody and returned home to her ranch in Acton.

Love, Betrayal, and Tragedy
MADALYNNE OBENCHAIN
(1921, Los Angeles)

"They drove for miles and miles, up those
twisting turning roads, higher and higher and
higher they climbed. And those Hollywood
nights. In those Hollywood hills. She was
looking so right. In her diamonds and frills.
All those big city nights. In those high
rolling hills. Above all the lights. She had
all of the skills. She had been born with a
face that would let her get her way. He saw
that face and he lost all control. He had lost
all control."

"Hollywood Nights" (1978)
Music and lyrics by Bob Seger

Madalynne Obenchain, undated
photograph. *Courtesy of the Library of
Congress, Print and Photographs division.*

Madalynne Conner Obenchain's physical beauty and charming personality captivated many men, including her husband, a college classmate, and a lover. The press would declare that Cleopatra's feminine appeals were nothing compared to Obenchain's. In five separate trials, jurors failed to convict this alluring enchantress of murdering her lover. But in the court of public opinion, she was found guilty of betraying her husband, duping the victim, and making a murderer of her college friend. Obenchain was a dangerous woman to be avoided at all costs.

The twenty-eight-year-old raven-haired beauty was well-educated and recently divorced. She and longtime acquaintance Arthur Courtenay Burch

Modern-day photograph of the Alexandria Hotel in Los Angeles.

Gravesite of J. Belton Kennedy at Calvary Cemetery in Los Angeles.

were charged with the shotgun murder of a prominent Los Angeles area insurance broker. Obenchain and the victim had been romantically involved for many years. The subsequent murder investigation, shrouded in mystery and police missteps, provided endless amounts of scandalous newspaper headlines for a curious public that never seemed to get enough information about the tragedy.

On the evening of August 5, 1921, twenty-six-year-old J. Belton Kennedy was shot to death at his vacation cottage in Beverly Glen, a rustic canyon affluent community nestled on the eastern edge of Bel Air. From the outset, the murder investigation was complicated by substandard police work. It was both aided and hindered by curious newspaper reporters who, through tenacious independent detective work, uncovered valuable clues but also contaminated the crime scene.

The sole witness to the shooting was Madalynne Obenchain, who had traveled west from Chicago in early July, stopping in San Francisco, where she planned to meet Kennedy. She told police detectives that they planned to get married in San Francisco, but he never showed. On July 6, she traveled to Los Angeles, where he lived, in hopes of finding out what had happened. She registered as a guest at the Alexandria Hotel on South Spring Street.

Speaking with police investigators, Obenchain reported that on the night of the shooting, she heard two gunshots and saw two men flee the scene but was not able to give a detailed description of the assailants. In very cryptic statements, Obenchain stated that she and Kennedy had not originally planned on visiting the cottage that evening, but things changed after they encountered a series of bad-luck omens. She explained that she was extremely superstitious and had pleaded with Kennedy to take her to the secluded cottage to retrieve a good-luck charm she had hidden beneath a rock on a previous visit. When they arrived at the cottage, she could not initially locate the charm in the dark, and Kennedy volunteered to go back to their car to retrieve some matches to better light the area. It was on his way to the car that he was assaulted and shot to death on the lower staircase leading to the home. The fact that Kennedy was not carrying keys to the cottage reinforced the belief that he had never planned on going to the cottage.

Obenchain also told police that while she was staying in Los Angeles she had been in contact with a married college friend from Chicago. Twenty-six-year-old Arthur Burch had traveled to Los Angeles in late July to help console her after Kennedy failed to propose. Burch was the son of a prominent Evanston, Illinois, Methodist pastor and was a star track athlete at Northwestern University. It was during college that he and Obenchain became close friends, but she was adamant that they had never been romantically involved.

Further investigation uncovered that in November 1910, Obenchain was granted a divorce by her husband Ralph Obenchain so that she could pursue a relationship with Kennedy. According to the victim's father, John D. Kennedy, she had been quite persistent in her romantic pursuit of his son, and from the outset he had been clear about not wanting to marry her. The elder Kennedy stated that his son seemed to be frightened and in a constant state of distress in the days leading up to the shooting.

In other developments, a neighbor of Kennedy's told police that about an hour-and-a-half before the shooting he had seen a car with dimmed headlights parked near the Kennedy cottage. The car had been obscured in some brush, and there were no occupants inside. It was later discovered by *Los Angeles Times* reporters that this vehicle had left distinctive tire tread markings, which led police to a specific Dodge roadster that had been rented from an auto livery business on West 9th Street. The owner of the livery identified Arthur Burch as the person who had rented the car under the assumed name of G. L. Jones on the evening of August 5.

A warrant was issued for Burch's arrest, and on the evening of August 6, he was taken into custody on an eastbound Salt Lake City train that had stopped in Las Vegas, Nevada. The next day he was returned to California while Madalynne Obenchain remained in custody as a material witness. During interrogation by Los Angeles police detectives, Burch steadfastly denied any involvement in Kennedy's murder. He told them that for the last two weeks he had been staying at the Russell Hotel, where he had visited with Madalynne Obenchain. Ironically, this hotel was located directly across the street from the offices where Kennedy worked.

During the investigation, police uncovered more than one hundred love letters that had been penned by Obenchain to Kennedy. These letters were considered very important to the prosecution's case and revealed all the heartache, joy, happiness, and disappointment of their relationship. The prosecution contended that Burch had stalked Kennedy during this period and killed him to avenge Obenchain's broken heart. Prosecutors insisted that Obenchain was aware Burch planned to kill Kennedy, and she was an active participant in the plot.

A grand jury was convened on August 10, and after two days of testimony, both Burch and Obenchain were indicted and charged with first-degree murder. Over the next several months, delays hampered the start of their trials, and eventually Burch and Oberchains's trials were separated. While the public awaited the start of the sensational court cases, newspapers were filled with salacious headlines. One such story revealed that Burch's wife, Allie, the daughter of William Quayle, a Bishop in the Methodist Church, had filed for divorce several months prior to the murder of Kennedy. It was alleged that he had abandoned his wife and son to pursue a relationship with Obenchain. These sensational newspaper headlines painted the picture of a saintly wife who had been rejected by a weak-minded husband for the beguiling beauty of a scheming seductress.

Then in early November, in a scene that would have made Shakespeare blush, Madalynne Obenchain was visited in jail in rapid succession by her ex-husband and codefendant, both of whom pleaded on bended knee for her hand in marriage. A bewildered Obenchain looked on with little emotion as both men professed their unwavering devotion and love while prostrating themselves, vying for her unreturned affections.

On November 22, 1921, after months of legal maneuvering by the defense, Burch's murder trial began with prosecutor Thomas Woolwine telling the jury that the defendant had stalked and murdered Kennedy because of the victim's marriage rejection of his friend Madalynne Obenchain. They depicted Burch as a vengeful would-be suitor of Obenchain who craved her affections and, with her voluntary cooperation, had planned the murder. Although prosecutors did not have a murder weapon, witnesses were called to testify they saw Burch with a gun case when he arrived in Los Angeles. They also introduced the tire tread evidence from the defendant's rented car, as well as the love letters between Obenchain and Kennedy. Prosecutors also took the jury to the Russell Hotel, where the defendant had stayed and allegedly watched the victim. Over the course of the proceedings, the defense called several witnesses to the stand who testified that the defendant was not in Beverly Glen on the night of the murder. They also called other neighbors of the victim who stated they did not see a car hidden away in the bushes near the cottage on the night of the shooting. This testimony struck a mighty blow to the prosecution's case.

In the prosecution's summation of the case, they began with a scathing attack on Madalynne Obenchain's character in which they depicted her as a home-wrecker, exploiter of male weakness, and a co-conspirator in the murder. Because of her actions, she had made a murderer out of Arthur Burch and a murderess of herself. They called upon the jury to save humanity from the clutches of these evil deviants and send them to the gallows. On January 12, 1922, the jury of ten women and two men began considering Burch's fate. After three days of deliberations, the jury was hopelessly deadlocked, and a mistrial was declared. Prosecutors vowed to retry the case.

Madalynne Obenchain's trial began in early February, and to satisfy a voracious reading public, newspapers were filled with columns and headlines that contained lurid details of the defendant's tearful demeanor and extravagant fashion sense. Prosecutors continued to depict the defendant as a woman of cold, calculating designs who had followed the victim to California, vigorously sought out his company, and ultimately conspired with Arthur Burch to commit murder, while the defense portrayed her as a victim of circumstance.

She took the witness stand in her own defense on March 9, and in a dramatic day of testimony, detailed her memories of love, passion, and tragedy. She continued to profess her innocence, her platonic friendship with Arthur Burch, and her original statements that identified two unknown men as the murderers. She also contradicted the prosecution's claims that she had been the pursuer in the relationship with Kennedy, tearfully telling jurors that on the day of the shooting, he had pleaded for her hand in marriage at a beach in Playa Del Rey, and when she rejected his advances, he became desperate and threatening.

Obenchain's fate was handed to the jury on March 17, and after only one day of deliberations they also found themselves hopelessly deadlocked with a nine-to-three vote favoring conviction. With no other choice, the judge declared a mistrial. A second trial was held in June, but the jury also failed to reach a unanimous verdict.

Arthur Burch was tried two more times with both proceedings ending in mistrials because the juries were unable to reach a unanimous verdict. Faced with slim prospects of ever getting a conviction, prosecutors petitioned

Arthur Burch's ashes are interred within the Columbarium of Compassion at the Mountain View Cemetery Mausoleum in Altadena, California.

and were granted a dismissal of the murder indictments against both defendants. Faced with what had been perceived to be overwhelming evidence, prosecutors had failed to win a conviction in multiple trials and encountered an outraged public who felt justice had not been served. Police declined to investigate further leads and suspects in the murder, which showed they believed the real murderers had already been apprehended.

Burch and Obenchain, who spent nearly a year in custody, were eventually freed from custody. In early February 1927, Burch again found his name splashed across newspaper headlines in Los Angeles. This time he was not the accused, but the victim of an assault committed by John D. Kennedy, the father of J. Belton Kennedy. Meanwhile, Madalynne Obenchain petitioned the court to retain her maiden name, became a member of the Women's Christian Temperance Union, moved to Laguna Beach, and tried to stay out of the public eye.

This all changed on July 19, 1944, when Arthur Burch, who had been employed as a fire department equipment salesmen, died from a heart attack in Pasadena at the age of fifty-one. In his will, he bequeathed his entire estate worth less than $2,000 to Obenchain. She instructed the probate court that she had no desire to collect the estate's proceeds and wanted the entire amount to go to the deceased's son. This story revived interest in the decades-old murder case, and curious newspaper reporters interviewed Madalynne, who maintained her innocence, professed that her relationship with Burch had never been romantic, and seemed bewildered as to why he would have left her his entire estate. After this episode, nothing further is known about Obenchain's life.

A Ghost in the Attic
WALBURGA "DOLLY" OESTERREICH
(1922, Los Angeles)

Fred Oesterreich, forty, was the owner of a successful clothing manufacturing business in Los Angeles. He and his thirty-seven-year-old wife, Walburga—who was commonly known as Dolly—had come to Los Angeles in 1918, from Milwaukee, Wisconsin. On the evening of August 22, 1922, he was shot to death at his Echo Park home on North Layfette Park Place. According to Mrs. Oesterreich, the only witness to the crime, they had returned home around 10:30 p.m. after visiting with friends. She told police that she went upstairs to prepare for bed and was accosted by an unknown assailant and forced into a bedroom closet. A few moments later, she heard four gunshots. Neighbors, alerted to the sounds of gunfire, rushed to the scene and found Mr. Oesterreich's body near the front door with a bullet hole in his forehead and two more in his chest. Dolly Oesterreich's screams attracted the attention of these same neighbors, who rushed upstairs and released her from the locked closet.

Echo Park home of Fred and Dolly Oesterreich, where Fred was shot to death on August 22, 1922. *Courtesy of the Los Angeles Public Library: Herald-Examiner Collection.*

Police were dispatched to the scene and discovered two spent .25 caliber cartridges on the floor near the victim's body. A search of the house and grounds found that no valuables had been taken, and nothing had been disturbed. Homicide detectives assumed that the murder was committed by burglars who had been interrupted by the victims' return home. Later that same day, police found a suspect who they initially thought had committed the murder, James Casey, along with a woman and four other men, who were found in a nearby house. Casey was arrested with a .25 caliber pistol and a magazine from which four bullets were missing. Although this arrest initially appeared to solve the case, it was later learned that the gun was not the murder weapon. Casey was released then from custody. Following this early lead in the case, the trail of the killer went cold.

Eleven months later, on July 12, 1923, a break in the case occurred when Roy Klumb—a young motion picture producer and close companion of Mrs. Oesterreich's—walked into police headquarters and told detectives that shortly after the shooting death of Fred Oesterreich, the deceased's wife had asked him to destroy a .25 caliber pistol that he threw into the La Brea tar pits. He led investigators to the location where he had disposed of the weapon, and it was easily recovered. The handgun had been partially damaged, and the serial number had been filed off.

Armed with this new evidence, police brought Mrs. Oesterreich into police headquarters for questioning. She denied any involvement in the murder of her husband and retold the original story of being accosted by unknown assailants. She acknowledged that Klumb was a friend and that she had asked him to help destroy an old handgun, but the fact that the caliber of this weapon matched that used in the murder of her husband was pure coincidence. Based on this evidence, the district attorney decided to press charges against Mrs. Oesterreich, and she was arrested and charged with murder.

After a series of long delays lasting until early 1925, prosecutors decided that there wasn't sufficient evidence to win a conviction and moved for a dismissal of the case. Oesterreich was released from custody on January 15, 1925, but this was not the end of the story. On April 7, 1930, a bizarre twist in the case occurred when Herman Shapiro, a one-time attorney of Mrs. Oesterreich and former live-in boyfriend, delivered an affidavit to police that busted the case wide open. He stated that Otto Sanhuber, alias Walter Klein—the "vagabond half-brother" of Mrs. Oesterreich—had confessed to him that he had fired the shots that killed Fred Oesterreich. Shapiro went on to detail that there was a secret compartment located in the attic of the Oesterreich's former home, where Sanhuber had lived and was cared for by Mrs. Oesterreich. He felt compelled to come forward with this information after being threatened by Mrs. Oesterreich.

Walburga "Dolly" Oesterreich (1930). *Courtesy of the Los Angeles Public Library: Herald-Examiner Collection.*

Otto Sanhuber undated photograph. *Courtesy of the Los Angeles Public Library: Herald-Examiner Collection.*

Armed with this new information, police located the secret room and arrested Sanhuber, who confessed to the shooting after hours of interrogation. He told police that he had met the Oesterreichs sixteen years earlier in Milwaukee and was employed at their factory as a sewing-machine mechanic. He became very close with Mrs. Oesterreich, and when they moved to California, he came as well. For the last four years, he had lived in an attic space above the Oesterreich's home, and this living arrangement was kept secret from Fred Oesterreich. During this time, he fell in love with Mrs. Oesterreich and helped with household chores and other functions during the day.

On the night of the shooting, he overheard a violent argument between the Oesterreichs. Fearing his benefactress might be harmed, he rushed downstairs with a gun and confronted Mr. Oesterreich. A wild struggle ensued between him and the victim, and four shots were fired. After killing Mr. Oesterreich, he told Walburga that they needed to make the scene appear as if the shooting had happened during a burglary. He instructed her to go into a closet, and he crept back into his attic hideout. He stated that the burden of keeping the details of the killing secret had weighed heavily upon his mind for many years. Subsequently, police arrested Walburga Oesterreich, and she was again charged with the murder of her husband.

Otto Sanhuber's murder trial began on June 11, 1930. Defense attorneys presented an alternative killer theory, and the defendant retracted his confession.

Sanhuber testified that he had been coerced and hypnotized by Herman Shapiro, Walburga Oesterreich's attorney, to admit to the killing as the only way to save the life of the woman he loved. He stated that he had been locked in his attic hideaway at the time of the shooting and heard muffled voices. He also named prosecution witness Roy Klumb as a possible suspect in the shooting, noting that he was a frequent visitor to the house when the victim was not present and that he had seen Wilburga and Klumb in numerous compromising situations prior to the shooting death of her husband. On July 1, the case went to the jury, and after two days of deliberation they convicted Otto of the lessor charge of manslaughter.

Then in another weird twist to an already strange case, defense attorneys asked for an arrest of judgment based on the fact that the three-year statute of limitations for bringing a manslaughter case to trial had expired. Faced with the facts of law and no other options, prosecutors agreed that the conviction should be set aside. On July 12, the trial judge agreed, and Sanhuber was freed from custody. Upon hearing the judgment, Sanhuber showed the first signs of emotion; with tears in his eyes he excitedly embraced his attorney. Then at the jail elevator, he was met with a passionate embrace of relief from his wife. Once freed from custody, Sanhuber disappeared into obscurity.

On August 5, Walburga Oesterreich's long-awaited trial began. From the outset, the prosecution had trouble with witnesses and jurors. They described her as a conniving seductress, who, over a long period of time, had brainwashed Otto Sanhuber into falling in love with her. The defense hacked away at the accuracy and credibility of the evidence. When Wilburga took the stand in her own defense, she tearfully stated that she'd had no part in the planning or cover-up of her husband's murder. She pinned the crime on Sanhuber but also stated that she believed he had done it without intent to do harm. On August 23, the jury began deliberating Oesterreich's fate. After three days of deliberations the jury was hopelessly deadlocked, and a mistrial was declared. Then on December 8, after four months of legal squabbling over a retrial, prosecutors agreed to dismiss the case on grounds of insufficient evidence. In the end, Fred Oesterreich's death was believed to be the result of a misunderstood argument between him and his wife and the lustful nature of the defendant's relationship, which forced them to conceal the shooting.

Then through years of legal delays and the statute of limitations, Walburga Oesterreich and Otto Sanhuber were able to avoid convictions. One major misconception about the case has persisted and needs to be clarified: Otto Sanhuber and Walburga were never proven to be lovers, although Sanhuber did state that he loved and cared for her. No proof of a sexual relationship was ever presented during any of the trials. These conclusions are pure fabrication, and although there is some circumstantial evidence that might allow the casual reader to conclude that Walburga did have several adulterous relationships during the period, these claims of a Sanhuber relationship have never been confirmed.

On March 24, 1961, Walburga married her longtime business partner, sixty-five-year-old Ray Hedrick, whom she had lived with for the previous twenty years. Fifteen days later, she died from cancer at a Los Angeles-area hospital and was buried at Holy Cross Cemetery.

In her possession was a three-page typewritten will dated May 20, 1953, bequeathing her entire estate (estimated to be worth more than one million dollars) to Hedrick. She had no other heirs, and her only child had died in 1910. This story served as the inspiration for two feature films: *The Bliss of Mrs. Blossom* (1968) and *The Man in the Attic* (1995).

The Tiger Woman
CLARA PHILLIPS
(1922, Los Angeles)

On July 10, 1922, Clara Phillips—a twenty-year-old former chorus girl, beauty queen, and Hollywood film extra—was distraught after learning of her husband's infidelities and went to a Los Angeles-area hardware store to purchase a claw hammer. She matter-of-factly asked a sales clerk if she thought the tool would be heavy enough to kill someone. Thinking it was a joke, the clerk replied that it would most likely do the job. Satisfied with the answer, Phillips bought the hammer and returned home. The next day she met a close friend, twenty-year-old Peggy Caffee, at a Long Beach speakeasy. Clara then told Peggy of her husband's affair with an attractive nineteen-year-old widow named Alberta Tremaine Meadows.

During the early part of the 1920s, when oil wells were springing up all across Southern California, Armour Lee Phillips, twenty-nine, was beginning a career as an oil stock salesman. Charming and handsome, he bought expensive suits and a big house, all on credit, for his young wife, Clara, whom he had married when she was a teenager. As Armour's financial situation turned dire, his marriage also began to deteriorate. As a result of these pressures, he turned to Meadows, a seductive young bank clerk, for comfort. Always paranoid and suspicious of her husband's activities, Clara began following him and soon discovered the affair.

After drowning her sorrows with alcohol all afternoon, Clara and Peggy went to Alberta's place of employment at the Citizens National Bank in

Armour L. Phillips, circa 1932. *Courtesy of the Los Angeles Public Library: Herald-Examiner Collection.*

downtown Los Angeles. Around 4:00 p.m. Meadows left the bank and walked to a nearby parking lot at 9th and Main Streets, where she had left her car. There she was cheerfully greeted by Phillips and Caffee. Being on somewhat friendly terms with Phillips, Meadows was unaware that she was in mortal danger. Fabricating a story, Phillips told Meadows that they had been shopping downtown and needed a ride to her sister's home in Montecito Heights. Meadows reluctantly agreed to give them a ride. The trio exchanged pleasant conversation along the way until they reached an isolated portion of Montecito Drive. Clara calmly instructed Meadows to pull over to the side of the road so they could discuss a private matter. After parking the car, the women exited the vehicle, and Phillips's demeanor changed dramatically. She angrily confronted Meadows, demanding to know her relationship status with her husband. Denying any improprieties, Meadows tried to change the topic of conversation and attempted to return to the car, but things quickly turned violent between the two women.

A physical struggle ensued, and fearing for her life, Meadows fled down a darkened hillside with Phillips in hot pursuit wielding a hammer. When Meadows stumbled and fell, Phillips immediately pounced, hoisted the weapon above her head, and began wildly striking the helpless victim until the handle broke. Assuming Meadows was dead, Clara returned to the car. Peggy Caffee, who witnessed the horrific events unfold, said nothing as the two women drove home in the victim's car. Homicide detectives would later describe the viciousness of the attack and condition of the victim's body as looking as if the woman had been mauled by a tiger.

Returning home with blood-soaked clothing and being on the verge of collapse, Clara greeted her befuddled husband, stating, "Don't leave, don't leave." Becoming more hysterical, she shouted, "I've killed the one you love best. You'll never see her again. Oh, I can't live without you."

In shock and not quite sure what had happened, Armour helped his wife wash up as she confessed to the horrific events that had just unfolded. Later that night, afraid of detection, Armour and Clara decided that they needed

Clara Phillips, the infamous Tiger Woman sits in front of her jail cell, 1922. *Courtesy of the Los Angeles Times Photographic Archives/ University of California, Los Angeles.*

Peggy Caffee, key witness in the case against her friend Clara Phillips. *Courtesy of Los Angeles Public Library: Herald Examiner Collection.*

to dispose of Meadows's car. Driving to Pomona late in the night, they left the vehicle near the Greek Theater and then returned to Los Angeles. It was further decided that Clara needed to leave town and would take an early morning train to El Paso.

She checked into the Biltmore Hotel under an assumed name and waited for morning to arrive. Armour, in a state of shock, wandered the streets overnight, not knowing what to do. The next morning, in a state of exhaustion, he dropped off his wife at Union Station and then proceeded to his attorney's office. There, he told of his wife's crimes, and the police were alerted. The Los Angeles Sheriff's Department telephoned Tucson police, who arrested Clara without incident when the train briefly stopped in the city. When she returned to Los Angeles, she was greeted by swarms of newspaper reporters and photographers, who soon dubbed her the "Tiger Woman" for the brutal nature of the crime.

On December 5, 1922, Clara Phillips escaped from the Los Angeles County jail. The arrows show her escape route. *Courtesy of the Los Angeles Public Library: Herald-Examiner Collection.*

On July 17, a coroner's jury declared that Clara Phillips had deliberately murdered Alberta Meadows, and two days later she was officially charged with first-degree murder. Her sensational headline-grabbing trial began on October 20, and throughout the proceedings that lasted nearly a month the prosecution called scores of witnesses, including Peggy Caffee. Clara had pleaded innocent by reason of insanity. Her defense attorneys called five psychiatrists to the witness stand, all of whom testified that the defendant had the mental capacity of an eight-year-old child, and that she was also susceptible to epileptic fits, which could account for her violent rages. She took the witness stand in her own defense on November 2 and testified that gossip about her husband's infidelities had driven her insane. She also claimed that Peggy Caffee had been the mastermind behind the murder, had arranged the meeting with the victim, and had actually struck the first blows.

On November 15, armed with this explosive testimony, the jury of nine men and three women began deliberating Phillips's fate. After two days of contentious debate in which a unanimous decision on first-degree charges and a capital punishment sentence could not be reached, the jury was able to reach a compromise verdict of second-degree murder. At her sentencing, a defiant Phillips, who was then sentenced to ten years to life in prison, vowed to seek a new trial.

On December 5, in another twist to an already sensational story, Clara escaped from the Los Angeles County jail. She was said to have cut the bars of her cell, hoisted herself onto the roof, and then slid down a drainpipe and vanished. But the truth behind the escape is less dramatic. In reality, Clara had bribed a sheriff's deputy with sexual favors to unlock her cell door, and she simply walked out the front door of the jail. A nationwide manhunt ensued, and dozens of false sightings were reported from Canada to Mexico.

In late April 1923, after being on the loose for several months, Phillips and two companions were captured in Honduras. In order to accelerate extradition to the United States, authorities promised Clara a guaranteed parole date if she voluntarily returned without a legal fight. She agreed to the arrangement, returned to California, and was immediately sent to San Quentin prison to begin serving her sentence.

In the spring of 1935, Clara was granted parole and released from custody. She could have been freed several years earlier but had gotten into trouble for penning sexually explicit notes to a fellow convict. By the time of her release, Clara and her husband had been divorced for several years. Shortly after the conclusion of the original trial, Armour Phillips returned to his native city of Galveston, Texas, where he continued to work in the oil business until his death in 1972. Alberta Meadows was buried in an unmarked grave at Forest Lawn Memorial Park in Glendale, and Peggy Caffee drifted from the headlines into obscurity.

As Clara exited the prison, she was greeted by her sister and reporters to whom she stated, "There is a great deal more kindness in this world behind bars than in the world outside." Phillips then moved to San Diego to be near her family. It has been alleged that she worked as a dental assistant for many years, a trade she had apparently learned while in prison, but this information was unable to be verified. No further information was uncovered about her life.

Baby Borgia
ALSA THOMPSON
(1925, Los Angeles)

L ittle hands moving swiftly in the kitchen. A scheming childish mind planning and plotting. Poisonous sulphuric acid taken from a radio battery and a can of ant paste stolen from a kitchen shelf. These things all worked together on the evening of February 2, 1925, when seven-year-old Alsa Thompson cooked a villainous meal for her foster family at their home in Hollywood, California. The dinner was so unpleasant smelling that Inez Platts, her husband, and two children refused to eat it. Then in a fit of homicidal rage, Alsa attacked her five-year-old sister, Maxine, with a safety razor.

Inez Platts told police investigators that Alsa had admitted her murderous plot and that she also declared she had committed similar poisonings in the past that caused the deaths of two sisters and her former caregiver. Mrs. Platts further stated that Alsa and Maxine had been living with her for the past two months. Their parents were unable to care for them after their marriage dissolved, and they left the children in her care. Alsa's mother, Claire, worked at a downtown Los Angeles department store, and her father, Russell, lived and worked in Santa Ana.

Alsa was taken to the local hospital and placed in a psychiatric ward for observation. Speaking in a whisper, she spoke with three doctors, telling them that she might continue her actions if she was released from custody. In a matter-of-fact and remorseless manner she stated:

> I poisoned my baby sisters by feeding them ground glass in some breakfast food. I wanted to see them suffer. They died in a few days after I gave them the glass. I put ant paste in food that was to be given Miss Nettie Steele . . . because I wanted to see her die. I put acid in the food at the Platts home because I wanted to kill them.

Police detectives interviewed everyone who knew the young girl, and they discovered that she was highly intelligent. Her teachers described her as a bright student who never caused any trouble. Police and physicians had never seen such homicidal behavior in such a young person.

Russell Thompson, Alsa's father, was vocal in defense of his daughter and branded her confessions as childish fiction, "I don't question the fact that she said what she is quoted as saying. I just don't believe that she ever did anything of the kind. Why. It's impossible." He stated that his twin daughters had died in Canada in 1922, from pneumonia and were under constant medical care. It was also confirmed that Nettie Steele, the nanny who cared for Alsa and her sister had died in October 1924 from stomach cancer and not poison. The doctors who examined Alsa agreed with Russell Thompson. They were convinced the young child had fabricated the whole incident and had an over-active imagination.

Los Angeles District Attorney, Buron Fitts was perplexed by the whole situation. "Frankly, I don't know what to think. It's the most extraordinary case I ever heard of. I don't know whether to believe the child or not. Her stories sound improbable, but then there is the way she tells them. I just don't want to think about it yet." Fitts wasn't the only one puzzled by Alsa's admissions.

On February 5, Superior Court Judge Walter S. Gates presided over the Lunacy Commission's questioning of Alsa. He declared that she was sane but lacking in judgment and emotion. He also ruled that she had made up all of the stories, and that her living environment had played a significant role in this fabrication. She was not charged with a crime, but was remanded to a safe haven home for psychiatric treatment.

At the conclusion of the hearing, Russell Thompson stated, "My child will now be allowed to get the proper care, and I am sure it is the best thing in the world for her. I think she is better away from the influences to which she has been subject, including her mother. I have nothing further to say. I will not capitalize in any way on my child." Russell further denied earlier reports that he and his estranged wife might reconcile. In fact, he filed a petition in Juvenile Court asking that his daughters be made wards of the court until he could be granted full custody. It was interesting that Russell included his wife as a negative influence in his daughters' lives.

On March 16, the courts agreed with Russell Thompson, because he was awarded full custody of both daughters. It was determined that Alsa's disturbing revelations had been the product of twisted suggestions by an adult. Whether these ideas had been planted by Inez Platts, or the child's mother, was not specified. After the ordeal, Russell Thompson and his daughters moved to Santa Ana, California, and settled into a normal life, away from the perverse influences of the Platts and their mother.

A Mother's Pain
EDNA MAY FULLER
(1926, San Francisco)

On the afternoon of September 2, 1926, a large crowd of curious and sympathetic strangers gathered at a San Francisco funeral parlor not far from Golden Gate Park to view the bodies of Edna May Fuller, thirty-nine, and her five children. Two days earlier, Fuller—after suffering a complete mental breakdown—had killed herself and her children at their basement apartment on Third Avenue.

For several months leading up to the tragedy, Edna had been experiencing severe bouts of anxiety and depression fueled by financial burdens within the family. Her husband, Otto, who was often unemployed or underemployed, had only recently started a job that required him to work nights. Burdened by the helplessness of not knowing how to feed or care for her family, Edna often awoke in the middle of the night shrieking and screaming. These sleepless nights began to take a deadly toll on her mental and physical well-being. Not wanting her children to suffer from hunger or the embarrassment of being thrown out of their home, she was determined that the only way to ease their pain and suffering was to end their lives.

On the evening of August 30, after her husband had left for work, Edna methodically tucked each of her children into bed and then set about the task of closing all the windows and doors of the tiny apartment. Resolute that life held no purpose or future, she turned on the gas oven, left its door open, and laid herself down on a sofa to await the deadly fumes that quickly engulfed the home.

Early the next morning, Otto Fuller returned home from work and was horrified to discover his wife and four of his children dead in their beds. A fifth child, eleven-year-old Winfield, was found unconscious but still breathing. He was transported to a local hospital, where an emergency blood transfusion was attempted but ultimately failed to save the young boy's life. A distraught Otto, suffering from shock, retreated to the home of his mother in Oakland to mourn for his family.

A coroner's inquest was held on September 6, and the Fuller's landlord, Charles Maurer, testified that alleged poor living conditions and his overbearing demands had not caused or contributed to the murder and suicide. These accusations leveled at him were determined to be groundless, and he was in no way responsible for the tragedy. He went on to state that in the six months leading up to the tragedy, he had witnessed Edna Fuller's mental deterioration and was convinced that the Fuller children had suffered physical and emotional abuse at the hands of their mother. Two of the youngest children had allegedly been locked in the apartment and were not permitted to leave. His concerns about the children's welfare led him to file a report with local law enforcement.

These distressing and senseless deaths touched a chord in the hearts of the citizens of San Francisco, and several anonymous donors stepped forward to pay for the six funerals. On September 3, in a solemn and emotional ceremony that was witnessed by a crowd estimated to be in the thousands, the bodies of the Fullers were transported to their final resting place beside one another at Cypress Lawn Cemetery in Colma. The cemetery had agreed to donate the burial plots.

Arsenic and Old Lace
MARY HARTMAN
(1927-1930, Long Beach)

A rsenic is a chemical element that occurs naturally in the environment in food, water, air, and soil. Since the beginning of recorded history, it was the poison of choice by those who wanted to eliminate political rivals and spouses or to collect inheritances. It was nicknamed the king of poisons and was infamously used by the Medici and Borgia families to kill their rivals; it may even have contributed to the death of Napoleon Bonaparte.

This poison was easily available to anyone through pharmacies because it was a common ingredient in cosmetics, medical tonics, and pest control. It is virtually odorless and tasteless when mixed with food and liquids. Thus, it was easy for murderers to slowly poison their victims to make it appear like a natural death. The symptoms of arsenic poisoning include abdominal pain, vomiting, diarrhea, respiratory problems, and severe joint pain. So unless someone got caught sneaking a suspicious white powder into food or drinks, arsenic poisoning was usually misdiagnosed as naturally occurring illnesses such as cholera, influenza, or pneumonia.

Until the early nineteenth century, arsenic was the perfect murder weapon, but chemists soon saw a need to identify its use for law enforcement. A reliable method was developed by James Marsh, and during the sensational 1840 murder trial of Marie Lafarge in France, the Marsh Test was thrust into the limelight, confirming the usefulness of chemical tests as evidence in the courtroom.

On the evening of April 14, 1930, fourteen-year-old Ruth Hartman of Long Beach became very sick. She suffered from a headache and severe stomach cramps, and she had trouble breathing. Before a doctor could arrive, the young girl had died. Tragedy was not a new occurrence in the Hartman's household. Ruth's brother, Henry, twenty-two, died suddenly in October 1927, and the family patriarch, Oluff Hartman, died unexpectedly from similar symptoms of those experienced by his daughter. At the time, no foul play was suspected, and their deaths were determined to be from natural causes. Initially, no autopsies were performed. The family matriarch, Mary Hartman, was left alone to handle the family's emotional and financial affairs.

Faced with three deaths in one family within a two-and-a-half year period, Long Beach law enforcement officials decided that an autopsy of Ruth Hartman was necessary to clear up any suspicion. Several days later, toxicology results revealed that there were lethal amounts of arsenic in the young girl's

Gravesite of Oluff, Henry, and Ruth Hartman (unmarked and to the right of Henry) at Sunnyside Cemetery, Long Beach, California.

system at the time of her death. The coroner then ordered the bodies of Oluff and Henry Hartman to be exhumed from Sunnyside Cemetery in Long Beach and tested for arsenic poisoning.

On April 23, the results of these chemical examinations were revealed, and it was determined that they, too, had lethal amounts of arsenic in their system at the time of death. That same day police detained Mary Hartman, who steadfastly denied any criminal knowledge of arsenic poisoning, stating, "I loved them. So how could I have killed them?"

Investigators observed her erratic behavior and determined that she was mentally incompetent to understand what was happening. The Hartman's two remaining daughters were also questioned, and they told detectives they observed both Henry and Ruth complain of a bitter taste in the drinks they were served by their mother prior to their deaths. Police also discovered that each of the victims carried sizeable life insurance policies with Mary Hartman as the beneficiary. It was also revealed that Mary was suffering from severe financial troubles and that a death benefit from her son's employer was about to end prior to Ruth Hartman's death. Based on these facts, it was determined that Mary Hartman was motivated by financial gain to murder members of her family. She was arrested and charged with three counts of first-degree murder.

On June 2, a preliminary court hearing was held and testimony from several well-respected psychiatrists testified that Mary Hartman was insane and not capable of standing trial. She was ordered confined to the Patton State Mental Hospital in San Bernardino, where she remained for the rest of her life.

The Borgia of the Sierras
EVA BRANDON RABLEN
(1929, Tuolumne County)

arroll Rablen was a very considerate husband. A disabled thirty-four-year-old veteran of World War I, he was unable to appreciate music himself, being deaf in one ear from a war injury, but he was always eager to take his exuberant young wife, Eva, to local dances so she could have a good time. For Rablen this often meant sitting silently as his wife partied and basked in male attention. One such occasion was on April 27, 1929. Carroll sat outside in his car while Eva danced the night away at a local dance in Tuttletown, a rural town in Tuolumne County, California. Around midnight she brought her husband some sandwiches and a cup of coffee. They chatted in his car for a brief period while he ate and drank before she returned to the dance. A few minutes later, the gaiety of the evening was interrupted by the blood-curdling screams of Carroll Rablen. Puzzled by his calls for help, patrons of the dance ran outside and were horrified to see him writhing in pain beside his car. He muttered to these baffled onlookers that the coffee he had just drank tasted bitter and then lost consciousness. A few moments later, he was dead.

An initial autopsy showed that Carroll Rablen had died from natural causes, and a tearful Eva could not shed any light on why her husband had died so suddenly. Most of the public and the medical examiner believed that the death was natural, but there were some people who were skeptical, and the case remained open. Chief among those who thought the death was suspicious was the victim's father, Steve Rablen, who considered his daughter-in-law a gold digger and opportunist who had simply married his son for money and a substantial life insurance policy.

In the summer of 1928, Carroll Rablen, a recent widower, longed for female companionship. He placed an advertisement in a San Francisco matrimonial magazine, seeking a wife who wished to live in the scenic beauty of Northern California's gold country. He soon began corresponding with Eva Brandon, a thirty-three-year-old single mother from Texas. After several months of letter writing, Eva moved to California, and in early April 1929, she and Carroll Rablen were married. He was ecstatic to have finally found someone to share his life with, and he spoiled his new bride in every urge and whim. But what appeared to be mutually wedded bliss on the surface was masked by a sinister lack of reciprocated affection by Eva toward her new husband.

Following his son's death and the determination of the coroner's report, Steve Rablen pestered law enforcement officials with his doubts and concerns. To get him off their backs, investigators reluctantly agreed to search the grounds of the schoolhouse where the dance was held the night of Rablen's death. After a brief check of the area, a small bottle of strychnine with a label from a local pharmacy was found under a broken floorboard. When police went to Bigelow's Drugstore and asked for the poison register, they found that there was only one recent purchase involving strychnine. On April 24, the poison was purchased and signed for by Mrs. Joe Williams. The pharmacy clerk would identify Eva Rablen as the customer. Armed with this new evidence, police arrested Rablen and charged her with murder. She vehemently professed her innocence and suggested that her husband had committed suicide.

Knowing that their case against Eva Rablen was circumstantial and weak, prosecutors relied primarily on the purchase of the poison. But they knew the coroner's initial report had determined the victim's death was from natural causes. This caused a problem, and they knew more evidence was needed to win a conviction. Armed with this knowledge, they decided another more detailed autopsy needed to be performed to determine if strychnine was in the victim's body. To bolster credibility, they asked Dr. Edward O. Heinrich, California's premiere forensic pathologist, to perform the examination. After several days of investigation, Heinrich was able to locate strychnine in the victim's stomach and on the defendant's dress, while police found trace amounts of the poison in Rablen's car and on the coffee cup. At this same point, handwriting experts confirmed that Eva Rablen was the same person who had signed for the strychnine at Bigelow's Drugstore. Prosecutors remained tight-lipped about this newfound evidence.

On May 14, Eva's pretrial hearing was held in Columbia, and to handle the overflow crowd a makeshift courtroom was set up outside the courthouse. When the accused arrived, she wore a tight-fitting brown coat and was led across the floor to the judge's bench. The hearing was short, with only three witnesses called to testify. Rablen entered a formal plea of not guilty, and June 4 was set as the first day of trial.

On the day her trial began, faced with overwhelming evidence and an overriding desire to save herself from a possible death sentence, Eva Rablen pleaded guilty to killing her husband. In a written statement to Superior Court Judge James Warne, Rablen admitted that she had purchased the poison at her husband's own request and that they had made a dual-suicide pact together, for which she lost her nerve. The judge was unmoved by the defendant's statement and sentenced her to life in prison without a recommendation for parole.

Eva Rablen was taken to San Quentin prison to serve her sentence and was eventually transferred to the women's prison in Tehachapi. Within two years she had applied for a pardon from California Governor James Rolph and three years later for parole. In her applications for release, Rablen stated that she had been coerced into believing that a plea of guilty was the only alternative to a death sentence and that she was actually innocent and had not understood the meaning of her plea when she made it. All of these petitions were denied by the governor's office. After 1949, there is no further information about her life behind bars or her possible release.

The Baby Blues
JOSEPHINE VALENTI
(1929, Los Angeles)

Pregnant women usually expect the days and weeks following the birth of their child to be ones of joy and happiness. But some new mothers experience severe mood swings and depression that often starts a few days after giving birth. This is commonly known as the baby blues, and if this melancholy persists for weeks and even months, it is called postpartum depression.

The history of this illness dates back as far as the writings of Hippocrates; however, the symptoms of postpartum depression were not officially recognized as a medical disorder until the late twentieth century. During the nineteenth century, when women experienced depression many did not disclose their symptoms, and those who did were often diagnosed as being emotionally irrational. Women who sought help were often subjected to a variety of unusual treatments with varying degrees of success.

Postpartum depression is quite similar to the kind of depression that affects many people but with one major difference: Mothers often feel guilt, shame, and fear of not living up to the stereotype of a good mother, and because of this, they become even more withdrawn, disassociate themselves from their baby and family, and become suicidal. In some rare incidents, like the tragic story described below, they become violent and homicidal.

Nineteen-year-old Josephine Valenti was a deeply disturbed young woman who longed for a life filled with fun and frivolity. Her life plans dramatically changed after she got married and had a child. She was a powder keg waiting to explode and secretly harbored a hatred for children. Seething with resentment toward her eight-month-old son, Dominic, she silently blamed the baby for ruining her life.

In 1927, Josephine and Sabatini Valenti, a twenty-one-year-old film studio laborer, came to Los Angeles from New York. They lived together for a brief time before marrying in the spring of 1928. They lived with his mother at her Moulton Avenue home, a short walk from Elysian Park. In November 1928, Josephine gave birth to a baby boy named Dominic. Soon after the child's birth, life at the Valenti home became difficult; the young couple argued constantly. Josephine became depressed and rebelled against all forms of motherhood, refusing to care for her baby and threatening to leave the marriage. She expressed an overwhelming desire to experience more worldly pleasures, and her anger was becoming more and more explosive.

On July 8, 1929, these emotions came to a boiling point, and with a cool, deliberate calmness she tossed a lighted match into her child's baby carriage and watched him burn to death. Police officers who arrived at the scene were horrified by Josephine's lack of emotion and steadfast denials of guilt, even though several neighbors, including a young girl, had witnessed the act. Later that day, after hours of intense questioning by police, Josephine confessed to deliberately setting her son's carriage on fire. She told investigators in a matter-of-fact manner that while giving the baby a bath that morning she'd had an overwhelming desire to kill him. Then after carefully dressing the child, she placed him in his carriage and wheeled him out to a rear alleyway behind her home. Determined to carry out her foul deed, she returned to the house and retrieved a match. Stooping over the carriage, she struck the match. Nursing the flame in her cupped hands, tossed it into the carriage. As the flames quickly spread to the blankets, she stepped back and watched until the carriage was sufficiently engulfed in flames. She then walked calmly back into the house and told her mother-in-law what she had just done. Following these disturbing disclosures, she was taken into custody and charged with first-degree murder.

Josephine's trial began on August 29, and for several days numerous witnesses were called to testify, including the defendant, who withdrew her earlier confession and stated that she did not know how the carriage was set ablaze. On September 1, the jury of seven men and five women began deliberating her fate, and after only twenty minutes of discussion returned a guilty verdict with a sentence recommendation of life in prison. While the judgment was being read, Josephine remained stoic and emotionless just as she had throughout the entire proceeding.

A separate sanity hearing was held a few days later in which defense attorneys asserted Josephine was temporarily insane at the time of the crime and that an operation, which she had undergone shortly after the birth of her child, had left her with dizzy spells and a reduced capacity to remember her actions. The jury failed to believe this claim and found her to be sane. On September 10, she was formally sentenced to life in prison. Whether or not she was ever released from custody is not known.

The Jimmy Valentine Burglary

MARY KAVANAUGH
(1929, Los Angeles)

O n the morning of August 19, 1929, the manager of the United Artists Theater on South Broadway in Los Angeles discovered that nearly $13,000 was missing from the theater's safe. He noted that there had been no forced entry, and the safe had been carefully closed after its contents had been removed. Los Angeles police detectives dubbed the case a "Jimmy Valentine" burglary after the main character of an O. Henry short story entitled "A Retrieved Reformation," about a reformed criminal safecracker.

The case was quickly solved the following day when an employee of the theater, Edward Kavanaugh, thirty-three, and his young wife Mary, twenty-three, were arrested at their Los Angeles-area apartment and charged with burglary and grand theft. Police and private detectives unraveled the case after tracing the stolen money to Mrs. Kavanaugh, who had recently opened two suspicious bank accounts under her maiden name. Bank officials positively identified her as the person who had made the deposits. When taken into custody, Edward Kavanaugh attempted to establish an alibi by declaring he had been confined to his home for the past week due to an undisclosed illness. He also steadfastly denied that his wife had made the bank deposits. After a preliminary hearing held on August 22, the couple was bound over for trial and released on bail.

The Kavanaughs met and married in New Orleans, where Edward had been employed with the sheriff's department. They moved to Los Angeles in 1926, where he found employment as a janitor for several businesses and began working at the United Artists Theater five months before the theft.

Their trial began on December 18, and prosecutors alleged that Edward Kavanaugh plundered the theater's safe while his wife stood lookout in the lobby. It was alleged that he had found out the combination of the safe while peering over the shoulder of the theater manager. Under oath both defendants denied any involvement in the theft.

United Artists Theater (1928). *Courtesy of the Los Angeles Public Library: Security Pacific National Bank Collection.*

On January 2, 1930, after two weeks of testimony and several holiday delays, the jury of six women and six men began deliberating the defendants' fate. After only three hours of discussions, they returned a guilty verdict of second-degree burglary. Both defendants received sentences of two to twenty-five years in prison.

At the time of her sentencing, Mary Kavanaugh was several months pregnant. In July 1930, she was taken outside of San Quentin prison to give birth and lived in a cottage just outside the prison walls with her child. On May 5, 1931, after serving seventeen months, she was released from custody. Her sentence was commuted to time served by California Governor James Rolph on the recommendation of the state prison directors. After her release from prison, Mary returned to Los Angeles with her baby. What became of her husband is not known.

CHAPTER FOUR

Infamous Criminalities of the Great Depression

(1930-1939)

"Women and birds are able to
see without turning their
heads, and that is indeed a
necessary provision for they
are both surrounded by
enemies."

—James Stephens (1880-1950)
Irish novelist and playwright

Beware of the Black Hand
ROSA TARLAZZI
(1930, East Los Angeles)

In the early morning hours of November 16, 1930, the alcohol flowed freely, and the music blared loudly at the East Los Angeles home of sixty-five-year-old Rosa Tarlazzi. The gaiety of the evening was shattered when gunfire erupted. Rosa's thirty-five-year-old son, Frank Tarlazzi, had been shot several times in the abdomen and stumbled to the backyard, where he collapsed. At some point during the party, a heated argument had ensued between the victim, his wife, Dorothy, and his mother, Rosa Tarlazzi, over non-payment of rent owed to the latter. When police officers arrived at the scene, they found Rosa intoxicated and in hysterics. She was following her daughter-in-law around the house, accusing her of shooting her son. Dorothy was still holding the smoking gun.

At the hospital, before succumbing to his wounds, Frank corroborated the story of a heated argument between the three and named his wife as the shooter. He also stated that she had tried to shoot him once before. Initially, Dorothy Tarlazzi told police that she was the shooter. Her story changed several days later at a coroner's inquest after a secret witness came forward and shook up the whole case.

At the inquiry into the case, Ruth Blescar testified that she had been at the Tarlazzi home on the night of the murder and named Rosa Tarlazzi as the actual shooter. Blescar claimed that she was in the living room at the time of the shooting "when from the open doorway leading to a darkened bedroom there suddenly protruded a long-sleeved arm, in the hand of which a revolver was clutched. Another arm, this one sleeveless, then shot out and the hand clasped the wrist of the sleeved one." Blescar identified the long-sleeved arm as belonging to Rosa Tarlazzi and the other as that of the victim's wife, Dorothy.

All of the other witnesses who attended the party claimed they were too intoxicated to remember any details. Prior to her testimony, Blescar had received several threatening phone calls in which the anonymous caller warned her against testifying: "Remember the Black Hand! The Mafia never forgets! And keep your mouth shut if you want to keep your friends!" These warnings took on a very dark and ominous tone for the case, and police took the threats seriously. Blescar was placed under special guard and had around-the-clock protection. Though these warnings were troubling, they did not deter Blescar from testifying.

Despite the sensational testimony from Blescar, the coroner's jury determined the shooting had occurred accidentally while Rosa and Dorothy Tarlazzi were struggling for possession of the handgun. Swayed by Blescar's testimony, the Los Angeles district attorney disagreed with the inquest's findings and obtained a criminal complaint against Rosa Tarlazzi, charging her with the murder of her son.

She was arrested and held without bail pending a hearing that began on November 25, at which time Ruth Blescar repeated her testimony from earlier in the week and added that she had actually witnessed the argument between the victim and his mother. Blescar stated that she witnessed Rosa Tarlazzi go into a bedroom followed by the victim's wife. She then heard Dorothy Tarlazzi say, "Mother, what are you doing? Put that down. Are you trying to hurt someone?" Blescar testified that she saw the victim walk toward the bedroom, and that's when he was shot. When questioned, Dorothy Tarlazzi did not remember how she ended up with the gun in her hand when police arrived. After several weeks of testimony and delays, it was determined that there was sufficient evidence to charge Rosa Tarlazzi with murder, and she was bound over for trial.

Her trial began on March 2, 1931, and when Dorothy Tarlazzi was called to the witness stand she testified that she didn't remember much from the night of the shooting but at some point had heard her husband and mother-in-law arguing in the bedroom. She then stated she blacked out and remembered nothing else from the evening. The prosecution's star witness, Ruth Blescar, followed and repeated the same story as she had in the previous hearings.

Throughout the proceedings the defendant appeared to be nervous and on occasion wept hysterically. Rosa Tarlazzi took the witness stand in her own defense and denied shooting her son, stating that she was asleep in a separate building on the property when the tragedy occurred. The defense also presented Frank Tarlazzi's deathbed statement in which he named his wife as the shooter.

On March 6, after four days of testimony and based on the evidence presented, the presiding judge reduced the defendant's charges from murder to manslaughter. Then after only a few hours of deliberation, the jury of nine men and three women determined there was insufficient evidence to convict, and Rosa Tarlazzi was found not guilty.

Frank Tarlazzi's dying declaration had exonerated his mother, and the jury knew that this type of statement was very powerful. In the end, the prosecution had misjudged the evidence in this case. The coroner's jury had ruled that the shooting was accidental and the case should have ended at that point. Rosa Tarlazzi was from a lower-class working family and was engaged in an Italian drinking culture that often turned violent. She was most definitely an integral part of the tragedy, but the jury found that there was insufficient evidence to pass a verdict of guilty.

Although she was acquitted of the murder of her son, she still wasn't out of trouble. Prohibition laws were still in effect at the time, and the use of alcohol was taken very seriously by law enforcement. Tarlazzi still faced a misdemeanor charge of intoxication; she pleaded guilty and received a thirty-day jail sentence. On March 12, her sentence was suspended, and she was granted probation and released from custody.

A Clear Case of Child Abuse
CUSTODIA VASQUEZ MURILLO
(1930, East Los Angeles)

When a young child is murdered, the most frequent perpetrator is the victim's parent or stepparent. Maternal filicide is defined as the deliberate murder of a child by the mother; and the risk of being a homicide victim is often highest during the first few years of life.

On December 19, 1930, two-year-old Rosa Murillo died at a local East Los Angeles hospital from complications of what was initially determined to be an infection. But treating physicians soon expressed doubts about the mother's explanation of her daughter's injuries and determined that the child's death was most likely caused by neglect and abuse. The child's mother, Custodia Vasquez Murillo, thirty-six, was taken to police headquarters and questioned about the suspicious death. She denied mistreating her daughter and claimed the child had fallen from an automobile several days prior, and it was these injuries that caused her death. Unmoved by her statements, detectives located several neighbors who stated they witnessed Murillo on numerous occasions angrily scold and physically strike her children, especially Rosa. Armed with this information, police arrested Murillo and charged her with the murder of her daughter.

Her trial began on May 5, 1931, and prosecutors claimed the defendant had for an extended period of time kept her daughter tied to a plank in a chicken coop at the rear of her home in Belvedere Gardens, a neighborhood of East Los Angeles. The prosecution's star witness was a neighbor who testified she had recently witnessed Murillo strike the victim with a milk bottle during a fit of anger. Defense attorneys attempted to refute these claims by calling a public health center employee who stated she had advised the defendant to restrain her daughter in order to prevent the young child from removing bandages from an unrelated hand injury. Custodia Murillo took the witness stand in her own defense and remained steadfast in her claims that her daughter's death was caused from injuries sustained from a fall from an automobile and not from mistreatment as the prosecution had alleged. During her testimony and throughout the proceedings, Murillo remained stoic and emotionless. While in custody at the county jail, she gave birth to a seventh child.

On May 8, the jury of seven women and five men began deliberating, and after only a few hours of discussions they found Murillo guilty of second-degree murder. Immediately following the verdict, the defense entered a plea of not guilty by reason of insanity and petitioned the court for a sanity hearing. These proceedings were granted, and after five days of testimony, the defendant was determined to have been sane and sentenced to five years to life imprisonment at San Quentin. There is no further information regarding Murillo's life behind bars, and it is assumed that she was eventually released from custody, but verification of this was not found. Rosa Murillo was buried in an unmarked grave in a potter's field section of Woodlawn Cemetery in Compton.

Poisoned for Profit
ANNA ERICKSON AND ESTHER CARLSON
(1931, Los Angeles County)

Courts in both civil and criminal trials use jury instructions, which are oral and written statements given by the presiding judge to a jury. These directives explain the jury's role and the particular laws that apply to the specific case. Jury instructions are very important and are designed to give jurors a framework for understanding how the law applies to the evidence they have heard during trial, so they can return a consistent verdict. Although in theory this is how things are supposed to occur, on rare occasions the trial judge commits errors in giving such directives. These mistakes often lead to unjust verdicts and full acquittals of defendants. In the following case, failed jury instructions would play a significant role in allowing a terrible miscarriage of justice.

On February 20, 1931, an autopsy was performed on the body of eighty-one-year-old retired lumber dealer August Lindstrom of Lomita. He had died at his home on Pennsylvania Avenue in the early evening of February 9 from what was initially thought to be natural causes. But after the deceased's son, Peter H. Lindstrom, raised sufficient suspicions, Los Angeles County law enforcement officials decided to delve further into the death. His body was ordered exhumed from Mountain View Cemetery in Williams, Arizona, and was returned to Los Angeles for examination. The results of the autopsy shockingly revealed that there were two-and-a-half grams of arsenic found unabsorbed in the deceased's stomach. The victim had swallowed enough poison to kill dozens of men. There were also trace amounts of split-pea soup found in his digestive tract. As a result of this damning information, Esther Carlson, sixty-one, a widow and longtime housekeeper for the deceased, was brought to sheriff's headquarters for questioning.

Carlson initially denied any knowledge of how the poison could have ended up in Lindstrom's body but implicated Anna Erickson, forty-two—a friend and neighbor of the deceased, who often brought food to the elderly man. Mrs. Erickson was taken ill the night before and had been rushed to the hospital suffering from what was later determined to be arsenic poisoning. The two women had drank coffee shortly before Erickson became sick. Carlson then cryptically told investigators that "She (Erickson) got me into all of this." She then refused to answer any other questions.

Further investigation revealed that several days prior to Lindstrom's death, Esther Carlson had withdrawn a large sum of money from a bank account jointly owned by herself and the deceased. It was also discovered that Carlson had given several hundred dollars of this money to Anna Erickson. A search of Lindstrom's home uncovered several incriminating objects such as an empty vial of poison in a sewing bag owned by Carlson and a crudely written will that had been recently signed by the deceased, naming Carlson as his sole beneficiary.

On February 24, a coroner's inquest was held, and after one day of scandalous testimony it was determined that August Lindstrom had been poisoned with homicidal intent, and it was recommended that Anna Erickson and Esther Carlson be held pending further action in the case. The district attorney then issued a complaint charging both women with murder, and they were placed into custody.

In a bizarre twist to an already disturbing case, police began to speculate that Carlson might be hiding an even darker secret. They began to investigate the possibility that she was actually Belle Gunness, a notorious serial killer who had allegedly murdered more than forty people between 1884 and 1908 in La Porte, Indiana, before vanishing without a trace. Many similarities existed between the two women including ethnicity and stature. But when confronted, Carlson steadfastly denied being the infamous killer.

The women's joint murder trial was set to begin in late April, but Esther

Esther Carlson. *Courtesy of the Associated Press Photographic archives.*

Belle Gunness and children, undated photograph, public domain.

Carlson had become seriously ill and was incarcerated in the prison ward of the General Hospital. It was determined that because she was too weak to appear in court the proceedings would be postponed until June 2. It was also decided that Anna Erickson's trial would be split off and begin in early May.

On May 6, Esther Carlson died from complications of pulmonary tuberculosis, and in the hours before her death, she asked to speak with prosecutors and Lindstrom's son. Before anyone could arrive, she lapsed into a coma and never regained consciousness. What secrets she might have wanted to confess were taken to her grave.

The day after her death, detectives brought two former neighbors of Belle Gunness's to the morgue to view Carlson's body, and both men independently identified the remains as those of the notorious serial killer. A photograph was found among Carlson's possessions and was identified as a picture of Gunness and her three children, who had reportedly perished in a suspicious fire in 1908.

Following Carlson's burial beside her husband at San Jacinto Valley Cemetery in Hemet, California, there were shockingly no further investigations into the connection between Carlson and Gunness. In recent years, several prominent genealogists and crime historians, through painstaking investigation, have concluded that Esther Carlson was not Belle Gunness.

Anna Erickson's trial began on May 1 with jury selection. Over the next several weeks of testimony, explosive new details of the case emerged. Prosecutors charged that Erickson engineered the poisoning of August Lindstrom to gain control of a joint bank account with Esther Carlson, his housekeeper. Testimony proved that she withdrew several thousand dollars from this account the day after the victim's death. Other evidence showed the defendant was in financial trouble, and the day after the victim's death had made a substantial payment on her home, which was in foreclosure. It was also alleged that when the victim's death became a matter of investigation by the victim's two sons and police were subsequently notified, the defendant, fearing detection, returned a portion of the withdrawn money to the original bank account in an attempt to cover up her connection to the crime.

Erickson took the witness stand in her own defense on May 11, and for the next several days she denied any involvement in the victim's death. She testified that on the day Lindstrom died she had visited him two times and on both occasions had urged him to seek medical help. She admitted to feeding him some apple pie and administering a sedative to help him rest. She also acknowledged that on the night of his death she was given a savings account passbook by Esther Carlson and was instructed to withdraw several thousand dollars from the account. For her help she was given several hundred dollars, but fearing impropriety she returned her portion of the money to the account the following day.

On May 13, after closing arguments in the case were presented, the presiding judge instructed the jury of seven women and five men to return a verdict of either first-degree murder or acquittal. After several hours of deliberation, the jury returned a verdict of not guilty. Upon hearing the judgment, Erickson collapsed in relief and was quickly revived by friends and relatives. She was immediately freed from custody.

Was the verdict in this case a tragic miscarriage of justice, or were prosecutors inept in their presentation of overwhelming evidence of guilt? Did the trial judge make a mistake in his jury directive, and would it have been wiser to allow a lessor verdict of second-degree murder or manslaughter to be considered? These questions will never be fully answered. In the end, someone got away with murder, and only two people know the truth. One was exonerated and never again spoke about the case, and the other took her secrets (whatever they might have been) to the grave.

Spurned Affection
NELLIE BURDICK
(1933, Berkeley)

Enraged because her lover said he never intended to propose marriage, twenty-six-year-old Berkeley resident Nellie Clarice Burdick shot and killed him. From the onset of their relationship, which began six years earlier, she had been abused emotionally and physically. By the spring of 1933, the pretty blonde was on the brink of a nervous breakdown. In a state of denial and delusion, Burdick dreamed that someday her live-in boyfriend would legitimize their relationship. She loved him more than anything else in the world, but this love was never reciprocated, and when the subject of marriage was discussed it often led to a violent argument. Her unhealthy obsession with her less-than-honorable boyfriend, who had no intention of marrying his naïve girlfriend, had deadly consequences.

Twenty-four-year-old Mario Rossi, Nellie Burdick's boyfriend, was not a very nice person. He was a tough Italian with a long rap sheet of petty crimes that included bootlegging. He was very clear from the onset of their relationship that he was only interested in sex and nothing more. Rossi often bragged to friends and acquaintances that he considered Burdick to be nothing more than a dumb blonde and had no intention of marrying an American girl. These stinging rebukes were often mockingly repeated in front of Burdick.

On the evening of May 27, 1933, after yet another violent quarrel in which Rossi "stalled her off" on marriage, Burdick snapped. She retrieved a pistol from her bedroom and returned to the kitchen, shooting Rossi twice in the chest at their Seventh Avenue bungalow. She then ran into the street screaming hysterically for help when neighbors discovered the tragedy. When police arrived on the scene, Burdick was still holding the smoking gun. She was arrested and charged with first-degree murder and held without bail at the Alameda County jail. She pleaded not guilty to the charges, defending her actions as self-defense.

No murder had been committed in Berkeley for over a decade, and the sensational details of the crime were followed with great interest throughout the East Bay area. While awaiting trial, Burdick told newspaper reporters: "I loved Mario and still love him in spite of everything. All this seems like a bad dream. Mario had ideas of going to Chicago to become a second Al Capone. He was getting a gang together, and he didn't realize the dangers of the career he had planned." She also revealed that Rossi's parents had interfered with their relationship from the beginning and wanted their son to marry an Italian girl of their choosing.

Burdick's murder trial began in early August 1933, and the prosecutors contended that the murder of Mario Rossi had been premeditated and committed because the defendant's love was scorned. They used Burdick's confession to police as evidence. In her statement to detectives, Burdick was initially reluctant to reveal the cause of the quarrel that led to Rossi's death but eventually relented, telling them, "We have been living together about five years. I broached the subject of marriage many times, but it always led to a heated argument. If I had been smart I could have seen that he would never marry me." She also stated that on the night of the shooting Rossi had again refused to marry her, and this made her very angry. She impulsively retrieved a gun from a bedroom and told the victim, "So you won't marry me, huh! Get ready, because I'm going to pull the trigger." And she did indeed pull the trigger, shooting him twice in the chest. She also added that she had planned to kill herself, but when she saw Rossi fall to the floor of the kitchen, she ran for help instead.

Burdick's public appointed defense attorneys argued that she shot the victim because of "spurned affection" and out of self-defense. They claimed that Rossi had been physically abusive to the defendant for many years, and she feared for her life. They also claimed that the victim lunged for the gun when it accidentally discharged. Burdick took the witness stand in her own defense on August 9 and attempted to rebuff the prosecution's allegations of premeditation. She testified to suffering years of abuse and repeated taunts at the hands of the victim and said that his refusal to marry her led directly to the shooting. Burdick stated, "The whole argument was that he always threw it up in my face that he would never marry me. That I wasn't good enough for him because I was an American girl. He thought he could leave me and do whatever he wanted with me."

Other defense witnesses such as the defendant's mother, Julia Steele, testified that her daughter was in a constant state of fear of the victim, and that she had personally witnessed several physical assaults where Rossi threatened to kill her daughter if she didn't keep her mouth shut. Several other witnesses testified that they had also overheard arguments between the victim and defendant, and that Rossi often accused Burdick of interfering with his criminal activities.

On August 10, after three days of testimony, the jury of four women and eight men began considering Burdick's fate. They deliberated for several hours and returned a guilty verdict of second-degree murder with the recommendation of extreme leniency in the sentencing. As the judgment was being read, Burdick broke down in tears and sobbed uncontrollably. Four days later, Superior Court Judge Fred V. Wood sentenced her to five years to life in prison. After the sentence was rendered, Burdick requested that a small signet ring she had received from Rossi be returned to her. The ring had been introduced as evidence by the defense. The judge granted her request, and she clutched the tiny ring and bent her head low, murmuring to herself as she slipped it on her finger.

Burdick was initially sent to San Quentin prison to serve out her sentence, but was eventually relocated to the newly opened Tehachapi State Institution for Women. Her time in prison was not easy, and in December of 1933, she had the dubious distinction of being the first inmate of Tehachapi to suffer disciplinary action for refusing to do unspecified work. She would be denied parole several times because of her failure to cooperate with the rules and regulations.

In early 1939, she was granted parole and sent to live with relatives in Los Angeles County. One express condition of her release was not to leave the county. Never one to follow guidelines, Burdick violated this condition in August, when she hitchhiked to Berkeley to visit her mother. After her arrest and return to prison, she defiantly stated, "It was all worth it. I hadn't seen my mother since 1933." It is assumed that Burdick was eventually released again from custody, but there is no further information after 1940.

The Enigma Woman
NELLIE MAY MADISON
(1934, Los Angeles)

Circumstantial evidence—which is defined as evidence that only indirectly proves that a certain fact is true—is a legitimate form of evidence in California criminal courts. Many guilty verdicts are based on circumstantial evidence. The phrase "circumstantial evidence" is probably familiar to anyone who has seen a courtroom drama in the movies or on television. But not many people understand the legal definition of circumstantial evidence or how it is used in California criminal cases. In the context of California criminal law, circumstantial evidence, which is also known as indirect evidence, means evidence that does not directly prove that the defendant is guilty of the charged crime. Instead, it is evidence of another fact, from which a person could then reasonably conclude that the defendant is guilty. The following case is one such crime and conviction that was built around such evidence.

Around midnight on March 24, 1934, a series of gunshots rang out at the apartment complex at 3516 Riverside Drive in Burbank. The sounds of the discharged weapon created a panic among tenants, and calm was restored only after they became convinced the shots had most likely come from the adjoining lot of Warner Bros. Film Studios.

Early the next morning, the body of forty-year-old Eric Madison, a low-level executive at Warner Bros., was found riddled with bullets in his apartment in this same building. His thirty-nine-year-old wife, Nellie May, was missing. Apartment manager, Belle Bradley, who had discovered the body, told police that she had seen Mrs. Madison depart alone earlier that morning after placing a "Do Not Disturb" sign on the door of their apartment. This aroused investigators' suspicions, and an arrest warrant was issued for Madison.

Two days later, police found her hiding in the closet of a friend at a mountain cabin in rural Kern County. A search of Madison's car found a .32 caliber revolver, a box of cartridges, and a receipt for two other weapons that had been recently purchased in Hollywood. They also uncovered a handwritten will in her purse. Nellie did not cooperate with investigators and refused to answer any questions other than to deny killing her husband. It was later learned that she had been married three times and had met and married Eric Madison, her fourth husband, the previous summer when both were residing in Palm Springs.

On March 29, a coroner's inquest was held, and it was learned that Nellie was an expert pistol shot and that her third husband, William Brown, a prominent Los Angeles attorney, had sued for divorce on grounds that she had once shot him. Based on this information, the jury recommended that Nellie Madison be held for trial. As the verdict was read, the tall, attractive brunette wept for the first time since her arrest and continued to sob as she was led back to her cell.

In June, jury selection began, and prosecutors questioned potential jurors on whether they would be willing to return a verdict of first-degree murder based on circumstantial evidence alone and if they could put sympathy for the defendant aside in considering a verdict. The defense also asked prospective jurors whether they would take into consideration the fact that every murderer must have a motive and lack of establishing such a reason might play an important part in their deliberations.

Witnesses for the prosecution included Belle Bradley, the apartment manager who found the victim's body and testified to hearing several gunshots and a woman's scream. They also used testimony from ballistic experts and attempted to call presiding judge Charles Fricke, a known expert in weapons. The defense objected to his testimony, which was upheld by Fricke. The defense attorneys began their case by attacking the prosecution's ballistic evidence and related expert testimony. They questioned this testimony even

Nellie May Madison during trial, June 7, 1934. *Courtesy of the Los Angeles Public Library, Herald Examiner Collection.*

though the murder weapon had never been discovered. Then, in an even more bizarre claim, they declared that the victim might not actually be Eric Madison. Several witnesses stated that the postmortem photographs of the victim in the morgue were not of Eric Madison.

Taking the witness stand in her own defense, Nellie Madison, in a cool, collected, and steady voice, also confirmed that the man found dead in her bed was not her husband. Because of her matter-of-fact and emotionless testimony and overall demeanor during the trial, the news media nicknamed her the "Enigma Woman."

In closing arguments, prosecutors characterized the defendant as a cunning and cold-blooded murderer who could not erase the evidence against her by claiming the victim was not her husband. The defense countered by claiming the prosecution had an unseemly lust for blood and admonished the jurors not to let circumstantial evidence cloud their judgment.

On June 22, the jury of eight men and four women began deliberating Nellie Madison's fate. Two weeks later they found her guilty of first-degree murder and sentenced her to death by hanging. As the verdict was being read, not a trace of emotion was detected from the defendant. She sat impassive at the counsel table, behavior that was seen by many court observers to be out of character for an innocent woman who had just been wrongly convicted.

The verdict was appealed, but the California Supreme Court affirmed the lower court's verdict. In June 1935, at the Tehachapi State Prison for Women, Nellie Madison created yet another stir when she changed the narrative of events. In a desperate last-ditch attempt to save herself from being the first woman to be "legally" hanged in the state of California, she relented and confessed to killing her husband. Her admission changed her image from a cold-blooded murderess to an appropriately wronged woman when she claimed her husband had tried to steal her inheritance and that she had caught him in bed with another woman. She claimed that throughout their short marriage her husband had been emotionally and physically abusive.

On the night of the shooting, in a fit of rage, he had attempted to kill her, and fearing for her life, she had shot him in self-defense.

Armed with these new facts, defense attorneys appeared before Judge Fricke, who was unmoved by the new revelations and upheld the original conviction and sentence. Undeterred, defense lawyers appealed to California Governor Frank Merriam for a plea of leniency. On September 16, this strategy worked, and Madison's sentence was commuted to life in prison. The governor gave no reason for commutation of the death sentence, and his true justification has remained a mystery. The news media blasted his actions as a terrible precedent that was tempered by the sex of the defendant and reported that justice tempered by mercy put the safety of law-abiding citizens of the state at risk.

In the coming years, Madison relentlessly sought a full release from prison. She used her pen and wits to gain freedom by inundating two succeeding California governors with dozens of letters and petitions. In March 1943, these tactics worked, and Nellie May Madison's sentence was commuted to time served by Governor Culbert Olson.

After her release, she married for a fifth and sixth time and settled into a quiet and uneventful life in San Bernardino, California. She died on July 7, 1953, age fifty-eight, at a San Bernardino hospital and was buried at Mountain View Cemetery. Whether on trial or in prison, Nellie May Madison remained the "Enigma Woman," a shadowy and mysterious figure much like those in *noir* fiction that was popular during the time period.

A Great Miscarriage of Justice
BERTHA TALKINGTON
(1934, Merced County)

On the evening of October 16, 1934, Lamar and Bertha Talkington were driving a deserted stretch of Highway 33, just south of Gustine, California, heading to Modesto when two masked gunmen forced their car to the side of the road and demanded cash. When they did not comply with the gunmen's demands, the Talkingtons were shot. Lamar, a forty-eight-year-old Watsonville barber, was shot three times with a .22 caliber revolver in the side of his head, in his right eye, and in his chest. Miraculously, Bertha, forty-four, received only superficial gunpowder burns to her face and arm. Following the brutal attack, she drove to a hospital in Neman, where her husband was pronounced dead on arrival. Because she had been injured only slightly, police began to question the legitimacy of her account of the crime. During a search of the Talkington's car, police discovered several unused .22 caliber shells, which puzzled them and aroused even more suspicion.

At a coroner's inquest held the following day, Bertha Talkington's account of the shooting began to show even more inconsistencies. On the witness stand, she contradicted earlier statements and appeared confused. Police also located several acquaintances of Lamar's who claimed he had recently told them he feared his wife was plotting to kill him. Armed with this information, the Merced district attorney requested Bertha be held in custody as a material witness, during which time police searched for evidence at the Talkington's home. Bertha was granted a temporary release to attend her husband's funeral and burial at the Modesto Citizen's Cemetery.

Over the next four days, detectives interrogated Bertha, and the pressure began to mount. Eventually, she cracked and confessed to shooting her husband. She stated that she and her husband had recently agreed to a divorce and were driving to Modesto to withdraw money from a savings account to finance a trip to Reno. Bertha confessed, "He kept nagging me to drive faster, and for safety's sake, I stopped the car and got out. He pulled a gun out of the back seat and shot me." She went on to say that after two more gunshots, she attempted to seize the weapon, and during the struggle for the gun it accidently discharged, striking her husband. She admitted to fabricating the story of highway robbers to protect her husband's reputation, claiming she did not want anyone to find out that he had assaulted her. She also admitted to hiding the weapon in a drainage ditch near Gustine. Bertha was subsequently charged with first-degree murder and pleaded not guilty by reason of insanity.

Over the course of the next few weeks, police investigators uncovered more curious facts about Bertha's past. Her first husband, John May, had died unexpectedly from a spider bite in 1922, and their two daughters had also died under mysterious circumstances: Hazel May, an infant, drowned in a bathtub accident at their home in Morgan Hill in 1915; and another child, Esther Talkington, age seven, had perished after accidentally setting fire to herself with fireworks at the family home in Yuba City. Although these deaths were extremely suspicious, law enforcement officials shockingly decided to take no further action in those cases.

Bertha's trial began on December 17, and prosecutors sought the death penalty. Over the next several weeks of testimony, they cited three motives for the murder: collection of insurance money, a secret affair with another man, and her husband's alleged domestic abuse. This final claim of spousal abuse might have been a mistake and could have helped the defense justify the shooting as self-defense. They called more than three dozen witnesses, many of whom corroborated the victim's fear of his wife's wishes to see him dead and contradicted the defendant's claims of self-defense. Prosecutors also used physical evidence and scientific experts to bolster their claims against the defendant.

On December 26, the gaunt, neatly dressed, middle-aged defendant took the witness stand, and for the next twelve exhausting hours, she tearfully testified in her own defense. She repeated her claims that her husband, in a drunken rage, had physically assaulted her and attempted to shoot her. In the course of their struggle for the weapon, it had accidently discharged and killed him. During closing arguments, defense attorneys criticized the media's relentless assault against the defendant while prosecutors claimed the victim had been murdered by a coldhearted and scheming defendant.

On January 1, 1935, the jury of seven men and five women began deliberating Bertha Talkington's fate, and after thirteen-and-a-half hours reached a verdict. They found the defendant guilty of first-degree murder and recommended a sentence of life in prison. As the decision was read, Bertha showed no emotion and remained calm. She was imprisoned at the Tehachapi State Women's Prison pending an appeal of her conviction. Her appeal claimed that serious procedural errors had been committed by the trial judge, including commenting on evidence, giving blanket support to the prosecution's closing arguments, and coercing the jury to reach a quick verdict. Because of these egregious errors, she was granted a new trial that began in early 1936.

This time prosecutors admitted Bertha had suffered abuse at the hands of the victim, and this disastrous admission led to an eventual acquittal of the case on February 12. Following the verdict, a defiant Judge Edward N. Rector, who presided over the first trial, called Talkington's exoneration "a great miscarriage of justice" and "waves of indignation are sweeping over Merced County because the widow has been freed." Six months after her release, Bertha married thirty-year-old engineer Harry A. Coleman. He was fourteen years her junior, and they settled in Concord, California, a tiny city located in the East Bay area of San Francisco. Bertha and her new husband were never heard from again.

A Plea for Help
EDNA BEATRICE MALLETTE
(1939, Los Angeles)

Crime scene reconstruction is the process of taking all available information, with a focus on physical evidence, to determine the facts and circumstances surrounding a crime, a suicide, or an accident. Proper crime scene reconstruction is conducted in three phases:

Investigation: The crime scene is examined and documented to determine what evidence is present without consideration to the particular meaning of any of the evidence.

Analysis: Individual items of evidence, or groups of related evidence, are examined to determine their individual significance without respect to how those items fit into the overall reconstruction of the crime.

Reconstruction: All evidence, including testimonial and documentary evidence, is taken into consideration to determine how the crime took place.

Crime scene reconstruction can be described as putting together a puzzle without knowing what the picture is supposed to look like and without even having all of the pieces. The more pieces you have, the more clearly you see the picture. In the following murder case, police used crime scene reconstruction as primary evidence to gain an initial conviction of the defendant.

On the evening of May 28, 1939, Edna Beatrice Mallette, a forty-one-year-old and semi-invalid woman who had allegedly been bedridden for several years, was arrested in connection with the shooting death of her machinist husband. Louis Mallette, forty-six, had been shot in the head and hand with a .38 caliber revolver at the Lincoln Heights bungalow in Los Angeles he shared with his wife.

Edna initially told police that her husband had shot himself as he stood over her bed. A search of the home failed to uncover the weapon, and after several hours of interrogation, she confessed that she had hidden it in another room. Along with the handgun, police discovered a pair of white gloves. This was important to the case because there were no fingerprints on the gun. When detectives attempted to reconstruct the shooting, they determined that using the events as described by Mrs. Mallette made it impossible for the victim to have shot himself.

At a coroner's inquest held several days later, Edna Mallette, in a rambling and often disjointed manner, denied shooting her husband. She testified that

Beatrice Mallette at her trial, 1939. *Courtesy of the Los Angeles Public Library, Herald Examiner Collection.*

on the night of the tragedy, her husband had come home drunk, retrieved the handgun, and accidentally shot himself in their bedroom. She stated that he fired the first shot into the wall and immediately dropped the weapon, which then discharged accidentally, striking him in the head. Detectives refuted these statements by testifying that the fatal gunshots (based on the trajectory) could only have been fired from the middle of the bed, where Edna Mallette had been resting. A neighbor testified that on the night of the shooting, she had witnessed Mrs. Mallette standing in her front yard, wearing white gloves, waving a revolver around, and yelling, "My husband has been shot." Based on these facts and circumstantial evidence, Edna was arrested and charged with first-degree murder. Because of her health, she was held at the prison ward of Los Angeles's General Hospital pending trial.

Mallette was ordered to undergo a battery of psychological tests to determine whether she was fit to stand trial. On July 5, she formally entered a plea of not guilty by reason of insanity and, based on the results of the psychiatric exams, was committed to the Mendocino State Hospital for an indefinite period by Superior Court Judge Arthur Crum. In late November, it was determined that she was sane enough to stand trial, and she was returned to Los Angeles. During her hospitalization, Mallette told two different versions of the shooting: one in which her husband fell and accidentally shot himself and another in which she had shot him in self-defense after suffering years of abuse.

Her murder trial began on January 9, 1940, and the following day the defendant took the witnesses stand in her own defense. In a soft and hesitant tone, she testified that she had been bedridden for seven years and that she had suffered years of abuse at the hands of her husband and feared for her life. The illnesses for which Mallette had been bedbound were never fully explained.

A sample of her testimony—"I was afraid of him and had bought the gun for protection . . . Louis had been drinking . . . he was violent and threatened me . . . I grabbed the gun, and when he tried to take it away it went off twice . . ."

She went on to state that on the night of the shooting, her husband had come home drunk, and when she asked him where he had been, he became enraged. She feared that her life was in danger, shot him, and admitted to fabricating the accidental shooting scenario out of fear that no one would believe her story of abuse. Later that same day, the jury of ten men and two women began deliberating. On January 12, after two tension-filled days of discussions, they returned a guilty verdict with a recommendation of life in prison.

During the sanity phase of the trial, various experts testified to Edna's mindset at the time of the shooting, the majority giving evidence pointing toward her sanity. In the end, the jury determined that she was indeed sane at the time of the shooting. Judge Arthur Crum sentenced her to life in prison and remanded her to the custody of the Tehachapi Women's Prison.

Following the verdict, Edna's attorneys filed an appeal, and on May 28, 1940, the California Appellate Court reversed the conviction based on prejudicial comments made by the trial judge. On August 29, after a brief retrial, she was acquitted by Judge Thomas Ambrose on the grounds of insanity. Shockingly, she was permitted to remain free pending a hearing before the Los Angeles County Lunacy Commission.

Over the next several months, Edna continued to fight for her continued freedom. She had to stave off strenuous efforts by her own family, who wanted her to be permanently committed. Although there was overwhelming evidence presented that she would have benefited from further psychiatric treatment within an institution, on December 6, these requests were denied, and Edna was granted an unconditional release.

CHAPTER FIVE

Sensational Murders of the War Years and Beyond

(1940-1950)

"Four things greater than all
things are, Women and Horses
and Power and War."

—Rudyard Kipling (1865-1916)
Novelist, poet, and journalist

An Unjust Sentence
BEATRICE MAY COX
(1940, San Diego County)

From an early age, Beatrice May Cox was a troubled but brilliant young woman. She was an honor student at San Diego State Teacher's College, graduating at the age of nineteen. Following college, she found work as an elementary school teacher for both Imperial and Los Angeles Counties, but the emotional stresses of life began to take their toll on the young woman. In 1932, her parents divorced, pressures from work boiled over, and Beatrice was briefly hospitalized after suffering a complete mental collapse. After her release, she resided with her mother and a younger sister, but their relationship, which had always been contentious, continued with frequent arguments that often escalated into violence.

On the evening of January 27, 1940, another violent argument erupted between Beatrice and her mother. This time the quarrel ended in bloodshed with Beatrice allegedly shooting and bludgeoning to death her fifty-five-year-old mother, Clara Cox, setting their home on fire, and fleeing the scene. Clara's body was found by firefighters after extinguishing the small fire in the garage of the home. Due to Beatrice's recent erratic behavior and because she was missing, police considered her a prime suspect in the apparent homicide. Officials thought she was probably hiding somewhere in the rugged ravines and canyons surrounding the home, and an army of searchers were dispatched. After several days, there were no traces of the young woman, and the search was extended to include the entire state.

For the next eight days, she miraculously eluded capture. During this time, exasperated law enforcement officials suggested Cox had most likely perished in the canyons due to lack of food and water, or from the elements. They even speculated she might have committed suicide, and her body might never be found. Police detectives, making a routine check of the Cox's home, discovered a broken screen door. Entering the tiny cottage, they found Miss Cox hiding beneath a pile of clothes in a bedroom. She violently resisted arrest and vehemently denied any knowledge or involvement in her mother's murder.

After being taken into custody and charged with murder, Beatrice was transported to the psychiatric unit at the San Diego County Hospital, where she was observed to be suffering from an acute form of dementia. It was also learned that she harbored deep-seated feelings of bitterness toward her family, whom she believed had treated her poorly since her first mental breakdown many years prior.

Cox told police detectives that she thought she heard a burglar enter the house on the night of the shooting and, fearing for her life, grabbed a .22 rifle from a closet and proceeded to investigate. Upon entering her mother's bedroom, she was confronted by her mother who had been silently reading. An argument erupted, and her mother tried to take the weapon. They struggled, and the gun accidentally discharged. When she saw her mother fall to the floor dead, she ran from the house in a panicked state of mind, and unintentionally dropped a cigarette in the garage, which ignited the blaze. She recounted that after fleeing the scene, she roamed the nearby canyon for the next week with nothing to eat until cautiously returning to her home on the night of February 2. At her arraignment three days after her arrest, Cox pleaded not guilty by reason of insanity and was returned to the San Diego County Hospital to await trial.

Cox's murder trial began on April 19, and the proceedings began with a bang when the defendant stood and began hysterically screaming that she did not wish to plead insanity and implored the judge not to brand her as crazy. Faced with a courtroom of chaos, Judge Edward Kelly ordered a week's continuance of the trial. Once the trial began again, there were no further emotional outbursts from Cox. She sat stoned-faced as the prosecution presented their case. Cox's attorneys offered no real plausible defense other than entering into evidence her original statements that she did not know how the gun had discharged and that she was basically emotionally unhinged at the time of the tragedy and thus could not be held responsible for her actions.

On May 14, the jury began deliberating Cox's fate, and after only four hours they rendered a guilty verdict of first-degree murder with a recommendation of life in prison. Jurors did not believe the defense's assertions that Cox was not responsible for the shooting because she did not know how the rifle had discharged.

The following day the insanity phase of the trial began with very little new information presented. After only twenty minutes of deliberation, the jury agreed that Cox was insane at the time of the murder. On May 18, Judge Kelly officially read the sentence of life in prison and ordered her remanded to the custody of the Mendocino State Hospital for the Criminally Insane.

In hindsight, the conviction and sentencing were quite confusing, considering that the defense's assertion that Cox was indeed mentally incapacitated at the time of the shooting was upheld by the jury in the sanity phase. Thus, it is difficult to understand how Cox could have been found insane but also held legally responsible for her mother's murder. A more reasonable sentence would have been not guilty by reason of insanity, which is exactly what defense attorneys had argued for.

Too Good to Live
and Too Young to Die
BETTY HARDAKER
(1940, Montebello)

O n the late afternoon of February 19, 1940, the body of a child was found in the women's restroom at a municipal park in Montebello, a sleepy bedroom community of blue-collar working-class people located east of Los Angeles in the San Gabriel Valley. The young girl had apparently been dead for several hours before being discovered by a female park visitor. She was found lying face-up with her clothing in disarray. Her head had been crushed. There was very little blood at the scene, and all of the wounds had been clean and were free of dirt. Police initially thought the child had been the victim of a hit-and-run driver, who had possibly carried the body into the restroom to hide it. The building was partially obscured by large shrubbery and would have made it possible for someone to drive near the building and disposed of the body without being seen. A neighbor who lived directly across the street from the park told police that around 1:00 p.m. he had heard the screams of a child but had not seen any other suspicious activity.

Montebello Park, modern day photograph and scene of the murder of Geraldine Hardaker.

Several hours later, the child was identified as five-year-old Geraldine Hardaker. Montebello police immediately began a search for the child's parents. Her father, Charles Hardaker, twenty-five, was located at his home in South Gate and was taken to the Montebello police station for questioning. He denied any knowledge of the killing and explained that he had been working at the local General Motors plant that same day. His alibi was checked by police and was corroborated by plant managers. It was also learned that he had been estranged from the child's mother, twenty-five-year-old Betty Hardaker, for some time, and her whereabouts were unknown.

The child's maternal grandparents, Samuel and Etta Karnes, were also questioned. They told detectives that Betty and Charles had been involved in a bizarre voodoo cult that believed in human sacrifice. It was also learned that Betty Hardaker, the mother of two additional children, suffered from severe mental health issues and had been confined to an institution for a brief period. Mrs. Karnes also stated that she had returned to her home on Spruce Street around 5:00 p.m., where she lived with her husband, daughter, and three grandchildren. Because Betty and Geraldine were not home, she became concerned and began to search the neighborhood. An hour later she was told that the body of a child had been found in a park a few blocks away. She and her husband went to the county morgue and positively identified the body as that of her young granddaughter.

The following day Betty Hardaker was discovered hiding in an abandoned cabin on an Indian reservation near Palm Springs and was taken into custody without any struggle. During questioning by police, she willingly confessed to killing her daughter. In a matter-of-fact and relaxed fashion, she stated that she and her daughter had gone to the park around noon the previous day and had played for a short period of time on the teeter-totter. She then took her daughter into the parks restroom, and was suddenly overwhelmed with an impulse to kill, and without a second thought, picked the child up and slammed her head on the washbasin and fled the scene. She stated, "I didn't hate her. I loved her. I loved her too much, I guess. I thought she was too good to live." After killing her daughter, she calmly walked home and halfheartedly contemplated suicide before fleeing. She then hitchhiked to Colton, where two men picked her up and drove her to Palm Springs. She confessed to attending meetings of a cult that believed God wanted its members to kill people. Betty also told police psychiatrists that she had been hearing voices for several months. She could not determine what they were saying, but they kept her up at night. The onset of these voices began shortly after the birth of her youngest child and after her most recent hospitalization.

A coroner's inquest held on February 23 determined that Betty Hardaker had indeed killed her daughter and at the time was also of unsound mind. She was bound over for trial and pleaded not guilty by reason of insanity.

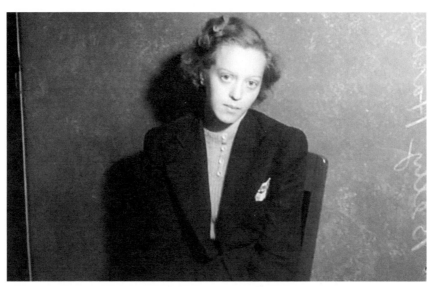

Betty Hardaker at the LA County jail. *Courtesy of the Los Angeles Daily News Photographic Archive. Department of Special Collections, Charles E. Young Research Library, UCLA.*

Over the next few months, numerous hearings were held to discuss her state of mind. During this time Betty's condition continued to deteriorate. On April 29, after several days of testimony, Los Angeles Superior Court Judge Frank M. Smith, declared that Hardaker was indeed insane and committed her to the Mendocino State Hospital for further evaluation. Eight months later, she was deemed healthy enough to stand trial and was returned to Los Angeles. Upon returning to the Los Angeles County Jail, Hardaker stated, "Why am I here? I hope I haven't done anything to make my family ashamed of me." During her incarceration, she refused to talk about her daughter's death and maintained that she remembered nothing of the tragedy, although she admitted to reading newspaper accounts of the case.

On February 11, 1941, after many weeks of hearings and testimony, Hardaker was found not guilty by reason of insanity and acquitted. She was subsequently deemed to have sufficiently recovered her sanity and was shockingly released from custody. In the months following her release, Hardaker attempted and failed to regain custody of her two surviving children. In May, she fled the home of her parents, where she had been ordered by the court to stay. She was later found near the home of her ex-husband in South Gate. Because of her increasingly erratic behavior, her parents committed her to a private sanitarium, where she spent a considerable amount of time over the next several years.

On April 28, 1944, Hardaker's bizarre behavior continued when she assaulted her ex-husband with an acidic substance outside her parents' home. She alleged that he had attempted to kiss her, and in order to fend off the unwanted advance, she threw the substance in his face. After a brief investigation, police determined there was no validity to her story, and she was arrested, charged with assault, and placed in the psychiatric unit of Los Angeles General Hospital pending trial.

On July 28, she pleaded guilty to the charges and was sentenced to ninety days in jail and three years' probation. After her eventual release, there exists no further information other than the fact that she died on January 24, 1956, age forty-one, from an undisclosed illness. She was buried at Rose Hills Memorial Park in Whittier beside her parents and a short distance from her daughter Geraldine.

A Bad Seed?
CHLOE DAVIS
(1940, Los Angeles)

Fourteen years before fictional preteen psychopath and up-and-coming serial killer Rhoda Penmark made her appearance in William March's 1954 bestselling novel, *The Bad Seed*, an eleven-year-old Los Angeles girl was held by police and questioned in the brutal hammer slayings of her mother and three younger siblings. Everyone who knew Chloe Davis thought the young girl was quite unusual, mature beyond her years, emotionally vacant, and not easily brought to tears. She was described by teachers as being a good student and natural leader. On the morning of April 5, 1940, veteran homicide detectives questioned the impassive young girl at her South Los Angeles home regarding the murders of her mother, thirty-six-year-old Lolita Davis, and her younger siblings—ten-year-old Daphne Ann, seven-year-old Deborah, and three-year-old Mark.

Investigators sat dumbfounded as they listened to a tearless Chloe matter-of-factly relay the horrifying chain of events that had occurred only a few hours earlier. The eleven-year-old girl stated that she had been sleeping and was awakened by the screams of her younger siblings. When she left her bedroom to investigate what was happening, she met her mother in the hallway holding a bloody hammer in her hand. Chloe continued, "She hit me on the head, but it didn't hurt much. I finally took the hammer away from her. Then Mama tried to set fire to my hair, but it wouldn't burn. So she lit her own hair. That did burn, and her nightgown burned off. Then she ordered me to help her drag a mattress from the daybed in her bedroom into the hallway near the bathroom." Chloe went on to state that her hysterical mother then laid down and said, "I've killed them, now you kill me. Hit me until I quit talking."

Continuing with her shocking tale, Chloe said her mother, in a rambling and often incoherent manner, had been pursued and tormented by demons and that she had been forced to kill her children to save them from eternal damnation at the hands of these evil creatures. Chloe then related that she dutifully did as she had been instructed and began hitting her mother on the head with a hammer. Nearby lay the body of her semiconscious younger brother, who was moaning in pain on the floor of the kitchen. Chloe stated that her mother gave her permission to put him out of his misery, which she also obediently did by striking him on the head several times with the same hammer until she was certain he was dead.

With the hammer blows not accomplishing the desired effect, Chloe's mother then requested a razor blade from a hall closet. Chloe stated she complied with the request; her mother used the razor to slit her own wrists, and she bled to death. The young girl's cool, calculated calmness unnerved the detectives, and as the questioning continued, Chloe described the aftermath of the bloodbath, detailing how she methodically cleaned up and then casually wandered to the next door neighbor's home to phone her father.

After several failed attempts, she reached her father. In a sweet and gentle tone, she told him, "You'd better come home right away." The neighbor who had overheard the phone conversation became concerned, but the young girl insisted she wouldn't say anything further until her father came home. However, Chloe changed her mind and told the neighbor: "It's something so terrible you'll probably read all about it in the newspapers."

When Chloe's father, Barton Davis, a fifty-one-year-old grocery store manager, arrived home he confronted his daughter at the doorstep. "What's wrong?" he asked. "You better go in and see," she replied. As they both entered the home, Chloe told her father to go into the kitchen. There he was greeted by the horrific sight of his young son dead on the floor while nearby lay the lifeless body of his wife. In another part of the house, Deborah Ann and Daphne both lay unconscious but still alive. Unable to control his emotions any further, he ran from the house screaming hysterically.

Chloe told detectives that she could hear him crying and told him to control himself and calm down. The police were called, and an ambulance soon arrived at the scene and transported Deborah Ann and Daphne to a local hospital, where they both died a short time later. Unconvinced of her innocence, officials took Chloe into custody and transported her to juvenile hall.

The following day, autopsies of the victims were performed, other crime scene evidence was analyzed, and police astonishingly determined that based

Final resting place of the Davis' at Woodlawn Cemetery in Santa Monica. Grave markers, Daphne (front left), Deborah (front right), Lolita (second row left), Mark (second row right).

Actress Patty McCormack as Rhoda Penmark in *The Bad Seed* (1956). *Warner Bros. Studios publicity photograph.*

upon the evidence, Chloe was telling the truth. The key to her exoneration was the confirmation that her mother had not died of a skull fracture but had bled to death from the self-inflicted slashes on her wrists. Newspapers and other media outlets quickly maligned Lolita Davis as crazy and demented. Chloe was taken to a secret location by relatives and spared the torment of attending the burial of her mother and siblings at Woodlawn Cemetery in Santa Monica.

Although Chloe had been exonerated in the slayings, she remained in custody at juvenile hall pending a mental health and custody hearing. At this hearing on April 24, Superior Court Judge W. T. Fox stated that because of the "emotional and mental shock from which she has not yet recovered," Chloe was made a temporary ward of the court, released into her father's care, but ordered to seek mental health care and not travel out of state. Eventually, this directive was lifted, and Chloe and her father moved to Cincinnati, Ohio, where they began a new life.

In the coming years, Barton Davis remarried, and he died on February 26, 1956. Chloe became a well-adjusted and resilient survivor of a domestic holocaust, married three times, and had one child. For many years, she owned and operated a successful beveled glass studio in Indianapolis, Indiana. She died on March 5, 1987, and was buried at the All Saints Unitarian Church

Memorial Gardens. She never again ran afoul of the law and was a pillar of the community in which she lived.

In 1956, Warner Bros. Studios released *The Bad Seed*, a film adaptation of William March's novel of the same name. The novel and movie are alleged to be loosely based on the Davis family tragedy. The film starred Nancy Kelly and Patty McCormack (as Rhoda Penmark) and was nominated for several Academy Awards including Best Actress and Best Actress in a Supporting role.

The Duchess
JUANITA SPINELLI
(1940, San Francisco & Sacramento)

Ninety years after the unwarranted and senseless hanging of a young Mexican woman named Juanita in Downieville, another Juanita was justifiably executed in California. Although they shared a common first name, these two women could not have been further apart in temperament and character. One was a victim of circumstances, and the other was a cold-blooded killer who harbored no remorse for her crimes or victims.

Juanita Spinelli was born on October 17, 1889, in Kentucky, and very little else is known about her early life. Nicknamed "The Duchess," Spinelli was the first woman to be legally executed in the state of California. She was the fifty-two-year-old mother of three adult children and the leader of a ragtag outfit of murderous thugs who roamed and robbed their way across a large portion of Northern California. Her infamous moniker was allegedly conferred upon her by fellow gang members who thought she had a royal demeanor; but to everyone else, this nickname seemed rather ironic, because there was nothing regal about her. Spinelli's entire life was built upon deceit, but she possessed the uncanny ability to influence the young and dumb to do her bidding. A con artist and ex-wrestler, she was described as a scheming, cold, cruel woman who could allegedly pin a poker chip with a knife from fifteen paces. She was a woman you most certainly did not want to double cross or disobey.

Over the years, she drifted throughout the Midwest and West and lived on the fringes of civilized society subsisting on menial work and con games to make ends meet. At some point in the mid-1930s, she materialized in San Francisco with her adult kids and a hoodlum boyfriend named Michael

Simone. By this time, Spinelli was a gaunt toothless woman who looked twenty years older than her actual age.

To appear more important than she actually was, Spinelli told anyone who would listen that she had once been an informant for Detroit's infamous Purple Gang. The criminal enterprise was originally a loose confederation of independent crooks, which began during Prohibition. Al Capone, the notorious Chicago gangster, chose to use the Purple Gang as a supplier rather than battle them for Detroit supremacy. During its heyday, the Purple Gang controlled all of Detroit's underworld, including the city's gambling, liquor, and drug trade. Nonetheless, the Purple Gang began to dissolve in the early 1930s through inter-gang dissention and warfare. By 1935, the coalition had splintered, and the gang no longer controlled Detroit's underworld. Because of the lack of verification and Spinelli's propensity to exaggerate her alleged connections, her association with the Purple Gang is extremely doubtful.

By the late-1930s, The Duchess—along with Simone and a handful of mischief-makers including Robert Sherrod, Gordon Hawkins, and Albert Ives—began robbing unsuspecting men and gas stations around the San Francisco Bay area. Spinelli's teenage daughter Lorraine was often used as a decoy, who would approach drunken men with a promise of easy sex. Once alone, Spinelli's henchmen would mug the gullible victim, stealing his wallet and other valuables.

Spinelli considered herself the brains of the outfit, and when she wasn't planning small-time robberies, she acted as a housemother, cleaning and cooking for the ragtag ensemble of youthful criminals. Acting as a teacher, she would instruct her apprentices on the finer points of armed robbery, assault, and car theft. She taught them that it was smarter to commit a steady stream of petty crimes than to rob a bank. Spinelli explained that law enforcement would go all out to find a bank robber but would more than likely shrug off the robbery of a bum with a missing wallet. She delegated tasks for the gang and doled out their cut of the money, as if it were an allowance.

The beginning of the end of the Spinelli gang occurred on the night of April 8, 1940. On a very foggy night in San Francisco, gang members Albert Ives and Robert Sherrod shot and killed Leland S. Cash while attempting to rob him of the day's receipts at the barbeque stand he managed at Lincoln Way and The Great Highway in the Sunset District across from Golden Gate Park. Fifty-five-year-old Cash was deaf and did not hear Ives when he demanded money. Cash reached to turn on his hearing aid, but a nervous Ives mistook the action as an attempt to reach for a weapon and shot the diner manager in the stomach, leaving him to die in the parking lot.

Returning to the gang's hideout on Golden Gate Avenue, the dim-witted duo told Spinelli about the botched robbery and shooting. She panicked and instructed the gang that they needed to flee to Sacramento. Along the way, they stole a car and robbed another gas station before finding refuge at a seedy motel outside of town. Throughout the night, the gang drank whiskey and planned more robberies in and around Sacramento. Much to the dismay of Spinelli, the dim-witted Sherrod continued to relive the murder of Cash, and fearing he might give away their location because of his continued ranting she knew he needed to be silenced. A plan was conceived to send the feeble-minded Sherrod on an errand so that they could discuss how to do away with their mouthy companion. It was unanimously agreed that Sherrod had to die, and it was suggested that they shoot him in the head and make it look like an accident, but Spinelli vetoed the idea. They needed to make his death look like an accident that wouldn't bring attention from law enforcement.

On April 14, 1940, while the gang was picnicking on the banks of the Sacramento River, Spinelli slipped chloral hydrate into Sherrod's whiskey, and once he was unconscious he was driven to the Freeport Bridge in Sacramento and dumped into the river to drown. The gang left Sherrod's clothing neatly folded on the bank of the river so that it would appear that the young man had committed suicide or had accidentally fallen into the river.

The next day it was decided that the gang would head to Reno, and they planned to rob hitchhikers and motorists along the way. But the real plan was to kill Ives before he also began talking. The plot was to kill him, take his body into the mountains, and dump his body where it would never be found. Sometime during the ride, Ives began to suspect he was in danger of being "rubbed out," and at a gas station near Grass Valley he ran into a nearby diner, through the kitchen, and out the back door and hid. He waited until the gang left before he went to a nearby California Highway Patrol post, where he confessed his story to stunned officers.

Later that same day, Spinelli and the remaining members of her gang were pulled over by police near Truckee. After the police found a cache of weapons, the group was arrested and brought back to Sacramento to face murder charges. In quick succession and in a futile attempt to save their own lives, each member of the Spinelli gang turned against one another. Lorraine, who was pregnant, claimed that she had been attending high school in San Francisco and was too busy with schoolwork to know about her mother's criminal deeds. She was held as a material witness and deemed a ward of the state. The city of San Francisco waived its right to prosecute Lorraine, but Juanita Spinelli, Michael Simone, Albert Ives, and Gordon Hawkins were indicted in Sacramento County for the first-degree murder of Robert Sherrod.

The quartet's murder trial began before Superior Court Judge Raymond T. Coughlin in late May, and prosecutors used the other defendants' own words against them. Spinelli had confessed, "I put the knockout drops in his

San Quentin prison booking photograph of Juanita Spinelli (1941).

glass. I knew they were going to kill him, and I didn't want him to feel it. Bob was a good kid." Ives, in an attempt to save his own life, testified that the other three defendants had been the masterminds behind the murder of Sherrod, while Spinelli and the others pinned the rap on Ives.

On May 28, the jury of five women and seven men began deliberations and the next day returned a verdict of guilty without a recommendation of life in prison, which automatically made the death penalty mandatory for three of the defendants. Albert Ives was found not guilty by reason of insanity and was not eligible for the death penalty. On June 4, Spinelli, Simone, and Hawkins were formally sentenced to die in the gas chamber.

After being held at the women's prison in Tehachapi and exhausting all appeals, Spinelli was driven to San Quentin two days before her date with the gas chamber. About thirty prisoners signed a petition protesting the execution of a woman and offered to draw straws among themselves to select a replacement. California Governor Culbert Olson granted her two stays of execution, but on the day after Thanksgiving, November 21, 1941, her time came. It was reported that she looked ghastly pale and wore a short-sleeved green prison dress while she clutched a white handkerchief in her left hand. Photos of her children and grandchildren were pinned over her heart.

As she was being led into the chamber, it was noticed that some of the sixty-plus witnesses were not in place, and Spinelli stood calmly outside the gas chamber and chatted about the weather as the remaining witnesses took their seats. As the guards adjusted the straps that pinioned her wrists and legs, she fixed her gaze upon an electric light just outside the death chamber. As the cyanide capsules were dropped beneath her chair, her lips pursed. She gasped five times, convulsed, and eventually lost consciousness. After five minutes, a prison official opened a peephole near the gas chamber and stated, "That's all, gentlemen."

Spinelli was the first female put to death in San Quentin's gas chamber. Even San Quentin Warden Clinton Duffy (who was not a death penalty supporter) said of Spinelli: "She was the coldest, hardest character, male or female, that I had ever known, and was utterly lacking in feminine appeal.

The Duchess was a hag, as evil as a witch. Horrible to look at, impossible to like, but she was still a woman, and I dreaded the thought of ordering her execution." Spinelli was buried in an unmarked grave at Mount Olivet Catholic Cemetery in San Rafael.

One week later on November 28, 1941, after eating a robust breakfast, both Michael Simone and Gordon Hawkins were led into the death chamber at San Quentin. Both men refused blindfolds and joked with guards as they were strapped into the seats side by side. Hawkins looked through the glass window and grinned at the witnesses while Simone only managed a weak smile. As the lethal pellets were dropped, Hawkins breathed the fatal fumes eagerly while Simone was a little less enthusiastic. Several minutes later the murderous duo were pronounced dead.

Albert Ives, the fourth defendant, who had been found not guilty by reason of insanity, was sent to live out his life at the Napa State Asylum for the Criminally Insane.

Mary Anna Took an Axe and Gave Her Daughter Forty Whacks

MARY ANNA COX
(1944, Placerville)

Fifty-five-year-old Mary Anna Cox was a very troubled and disturbed woman. She was born in 1888, and was married twice, first to Clay Ravenscroft, with whom she would have three children. The marriage ended in divorce. She then married Charles Kenneth Cox. This second marriage resulted in the birth of a daughter, Winnifred May Cox, in 1930. The family settled in the tiny town of Diamond Springs, California, a few miles south of Placerville. Mary Anna had struggled with mental illness all of her life and was hospitalized for three weeks during the early summer of 1944.

On the morning of September 15, 1944, while her husband, Charles, was at work, Mary Anna, for unknown reasons, attacked her fourteen-year-old daughter as the young girl was taking a bath and preparing to go to school. Mary Anna first struck Winnifred with a club, then attempted to shoot her with a .30 caliber rifle, but the weapon jammed. Retrieving a small camp ax, she returned to the bathroom and renewed her attack, slashing Winnifred numerous times about the head, which sent the teenager into a state of semi-consciousness.

Believing the attack was over after her mother withdrew for a second time, the young girl sat naked, dazed, and bleeding severely, unable to comprehend what had just happened. A short time later, Mary Anna's mood changed radically, and she went from being a homicidal maniac to a kind and caring mother. She gingerly helped her daughter out of the tub, placed her on a bed, and dressed the wounds she had just inflicted. A few minutes later, when her mother was in another part of the house, Winnifred, having regained enough awareness to understand that her life was still in mortal danger, crept silently into the hallway to retrieve a shotgun from a closet. Not wanting to alert her mother, she tiptoed into the kitchen and without a word raised the weapon to her mother's head and pulled the trigger, killing her instantly. Weak from the beating and loss of blood, Winnifred then collapsed on the living room sofa. Later that day, when her father returned home for lunch from his job at a local lumber mill, he horrifyingly discovered his daughter unconscious and his wife dead. He telephoned the local sheriff, and Winnifred was taken to a local hospital, where she told what had occurred.

After several days of recuperation, Winnifred was released from the hospital. It was soon learned that in the days leading up to the incident, the severely depressed Mary Anna Cox had apparently attempted to persuade her daughter to join her in a suicide pact. After careful analysis of the evidence and medical records of the deceased, law enforcement officials concluded that the shooting death was justifiable, and no charges were filed. What happened to Winnifred and Charles Cox after the tragic shooting death is not known. Mary Anna Cox was buried in a common grave at Saint Patrick Cemetery in Placerville.

A Shakespearean Tragedy
ANNIE IRENE MANSFELDT
(1945, San Francisco)

Somnolentia is a condition in which a person has an overriding need for sleep, or desire to sleep for extraordinarily long periods of time. It has distinctive meanings and causes, and the condition of being in a constant state of lethargy can be a symptom of other serious health problems. Symptoms include excessive fatigue, feeblemindedness, and a general lack of rational awareness. Somnolentia would play a significant role in the legal defense of the defendant in the following case.

Franz Liszt with his students, 1884. Liszt is seated in second row center, Hugo Mansfeldt is standing in the second row on the right. *Public domain photograph.*

On October 4, 1945, San Francisco socialite, former beauty queen, and aspiring stage actress Annie Irene Mansfeldt was severely distressed and depressed over her husband's alleged infidelities. She had finally reached a breaking point and needed to confront his alleged mistress. The forty-six-year-old auburn-haired beauty was the wife of prominent area physician John Mansfeldt, grandson of celebrated pianist Hugo Mansfeldt, a protégé of legendary composer Franz Liszt. As Annie drove the short distance to Vada Martin's apartment on Geary Street, her anger intensified.

Martin, thirty-six, was an attractive brunette and the wife of a navy man stationed in the Pacific. She was a longtime employee at John Mansfeldt's medical office, and she must have known something was terribly wrong because she at first refused to allow Annie Mansfeldt entrance to her apartment. After several minutes of cordial but extremely awkward conversation through the apartment's intercom, Vada reluctantly agreed to meet Annie Mansfeldt in the lobby of the apartment. Outside, Annie convinced Martin that they would have more privacy to talk in her car, which was parked a short distance away at the corner of Leavenworth and Geary. Once inside the vehicle, the situation quickly became volatile.

Getting right to the point, Mansfeldt angrily queried Martin about her intentions and feelings for her husband. Martin, who was taken aback by the tone of the questions, replied that she admired Dr. Mansfeldt and thought he was one of the finest men in the world but denied having an affair. This infuriated Annie, who knew the woman was lying, and in an ill-advised attempt to frighten Martin, she reached for a handgun. The weapon hidden just below the driver's seat had been recently used in a theatrical production and was thought to hold only blanks. She menacingly pointed the gun at Martin's chest and fired. But when Martin slumped forward, Mansfeldt knew immediately that the woman was seriously hurt. With her dying breath, Vada Martin continued to deny any improprieties, and these statements convinced Mansfeldt that she had made a terrible mistake. She started the car and drove as fast as she could to a local hospital, where she rushed into the emergency room, dropped the weapon on the counter, and loudly announced, "A woman is dying in the front seat of my automobile."

Hospital attendants rushed to the vehicle and found Martin slumped over the front seat, already deceased. As her body was being brought inside the hospital, a panic-stricken Mansfeldt collapsed. Regaining consciousness a short time later and after being placed into police custody, she mumbled to detectives, "Oh my poor children. My poor beautiful children. Now I know it was horrible to suspect my husband. He's so fine. He'll never stand for this . . . never."

John Mansfeldt was informed of what had happened, and he hurried to the hospital, and after briefly speaking with his wife, he simply walked away from the hospital. The next day, Annie instinctively knew something was terribly wrong when he failed to appear at her arraignment hearing. She feared that her husband most likely had already done harm to himself, and the police issued an all-points bulletin to bring him in for questioning. Annie's concerns and assumptions tragically proved to be true three days later when John Mansfeldt's body was found nineteen miles south of San Francisco, near the Shelter Cove Resort. Mansfeldt was slumped over in the front seat of his sedan, which was parked at the top of a cliff overlooking the Pacific Ocean. He had been dead for several days, and several empty containers were found strewn around the inside of the vehicle. There was no suicide note, and an autopsy performed several days later confirmed he had died from a self-induced overdose of morphine.

Annie Mansfeldt never denied shooting Vada Martin, but in an unusual turn of events she made a double plea: not guilty and not guilty by reason of insanity. Her attorneys then began leaking information to the press that helped plant seeds of reasonable doubt into the minds of the public and potential jurors. They pointed out that there had been a possible struggle for the weapon, and police erred when they had failed to test the weapon for both women's fingerprints. It was also pointed out that at the time of the shooting, Annie Mansfeldt was suffering from diminished mental capacity, which was characterized as "somnolentia" or "white fog" due to overuse of sedatives.

Photo of Annie Mansfeldt. *Courtesy of the Acme Photo Bureau.*

Mansfeldt's murder trial began on November 26 before Judge Edward Murphy. The supercharged energy of the proceedings was fueled by the general public's voracious need for information on the case, which was continually fed by an overzealous media and sensational newspaper headlines. On the first day of the proceedings, Judge Murphy made an odd opening statement in which he sternly instructed the prosecution and defense to use "an economy of words" to help move the proceedings along expeditiously and as smoothly as possible.

As the trial progressed, the proceedings took on a surreal atmosphere characterized as "topsy-turvy," with both prosecutors and defense attorneys often using the same witnesses to bolster each side's evidence. Several witnesses testified that they had firsthand knowledge of the affair between Dr. Mansfeldt and the victim. A defense psychiatrist also testified that the defendant suffered from a split personality. Her two young children were also called to testify; they told of their mother's odd behavior in the days leading up to the shooting and that their parents had also been fighting.

On December 4, a visibly anxious Annie Mansfeldt took the witnesses stand in her own defense. Prosecutors hoped that her theatrical background would not adversely affect the jury's ability to see the truth in her testimony. In forty-five minutes of riveting testimony, Mansfeldt acknowledged that she had tried to commit suicide several times in the past and that she had been emotionally and physically abused by her grandmother as a young child. She stated that the "dark shadow of insanity" had always been a part of her life. Although she remained calm during most of her testimony, she broke down in tears when she was asked to describe the mounting suspicions of her husband's infidelity that led to Vada Martin's death. Then gesturing dramatically for emphasis, she insisted that she had no memory of the shooting, which conformed perfectly to the defense's claims that she had been in a state of diminished capacity at the time of the shooting and was unaware of what had happened. During summation of the case, defense attorneys stated that "in the subconscious mind of Annie Irene Mansfeldt, there were evil demons," and because of this, she should be freed of the charges.

On December 19, the jury of six men and six women began deliberating Mansfeldt's fate, and after only four-and-a-half hours of discussion, they found her guilty of the lesser charge of manslaughter. A visibly shaken and stunned Mansfeldt nearly collapsed as the verdict was read.

The second chapter of her trial, the sanity phase, began several weeks later. On January 2, 1946, the first day of testimony, Mansfeldt was removed from the courtroom after hysterically objecting to statements by the prosecution. They had been vigorously challenging the defense's claims that Mrs. Mansfeldt had been driven to shoot Vada Martin because of insanity due to her husband's own mental illness and his numerous affairs. Jumping to her feet, she yelled that prosecutors were "not telling the truth" and that she "can't stand anymore."

Lead prosecutor Norman Elkington stated, "Mrs. Mansfeldt spent a good deal of time telling us about her motives. The doctrine of irresistible impulse is not sanctioned by California law, and anger, passion, and emotional disturbance does not constitute insanity."

After only one day of testimony, the same jury that had already convicted Mansfeldt of manslaughter began deliberating her sanity. On January 4, after eight-and-a-half hours of discussions, they determined that Mansfeldt was indeed sane at the time of the shooting death of Vada Martin. As her attorney waived any delay in sentencing, she sat subdued and composed as the verdict was rendered. Judge Murphy then immediately sentenced her to a term of one to ten years in state prison. The following day, Mansfeldt bade her children a tearful good-bye prior to being transported to the Tehachapi State Prison for Women. Urging them not to worry, "because that won't be good for my morale . . . I will be home with you as soon as I can; please don't forget me." Tears flowing down the children's faces, they promised to think of her "every moment."

On February 17, 1948, after serving two years in prison Mansfeldt was granted parole. Upon her release, she stated, "I feel just fine and am anxious to get to San Francisco, where I can be reunited with my children. My plans for the future are to lead a normal life and reestablish a home for the children somewhere in the Bay area. I feel I have paid my debt to society."

Although Mansfeldt wished to fade into obscurity, this was not to be. In February 1949, Vada Martin's husband, Wilbur, won a civil judgment against Mansfeldt for wrongful death and was awarded $35,000 in damages. Over the next decade, they fought over payment of these damages, which were never fully paid due to Mansfeldt's declaration of bankruptcy. During these proceedings it was alleged that she had transferred nearly $100,000 to a secret out-of-state bank account, but these allegations were never proven. No further information about Mansfeldt's life was uncovered after the late 1950s.

Murder on the Yacht
BEULAH OVERELL
(1947, Newport Beach)

The use of cameras and other media recording devices are commonplace in criminal trials in modern society. But seventy-five years ago, radio played a vital role in bringing high-profile crime cases into the living rooms of average citizens across the country. Millions of people sat riveted to their radios day after day as real-life legal dramas and tragedies unfolded.

The Scopes Monkey Trial of 1925 was the first nationally broadcast criminal trial in American history. The defendant, John Scopes, was a high school teacher, who was accused of violating Tennessee's Butler Act, which had made it unlawful to teach human evolution in any state-funded school. The trial was deliberately staged to attract publicity to the small town of Dayton, Tennessee, where it was held. Scopes was found guilty, but the verdict was overturned on a technicality. The trial served its purpose of drawing intense publicity, as national reporters flocked to Dayton to cover the big-name lawyers who had agreed to represent each side. William Jennings Bryan, three-time presidential candidate, argued for the prosecution, while Clarence Darrow, the famed defense attorney, spoke for Scopes.

By 1947, radio stations had been transmitting sensational crime trials across the country for more than twenty years, but its use in the following criminal case would prove pivotal in its eventual outcome and in the poll of public opinion.

Around 11:00 p.m. on March 15, 1947, seventeen-year-old Beulah Louise Overell and her sweetheart, twenty-one-year-old George "Bud" Gollum, left her parents' yacht, the *Mary E.*, which was moored off of B Street near Balboa pier in Newport Harbor. Their mission was to find a late-night snack. The elder Overells—Walter, sixty-two, and Beulah, fifty-seven—stayed on board their boat as the young lovers left to get hamburgers at a local diner.

When the young couple returned to the pier, they were met with a sight that sent them into shock. The *Mary E.* was smoldering and sinking. Coincidentally, at the same moment that Beulah had been ordering hamburgers, her parents' forty-seven-foot luxury cruiser had been rocked by a massive explosion. Beulah, her boyfriend, and others frantically called out for her parents as the ship quickly filled with water and sank. The bodies of the elder Overells would not be recovered until early the next morning when the Coast Guard towed the boat to shallow water.

Walter and Beulah Overell were wealthy socialites who lived in Flintridge,

California. Walter Overell made his original fortune in the furniture business in the 1930s and early 1940s, and followed that with successful investments in real estate. The Overells had one child, a daughter named Beulah Louise. People who knew the family said that she, like many children of wealthy parents, had been spoiled and overprotected. At the age of seventeen, Beulah Louise, a freshman at the University of Southern California, decided that she wanted a boyfriend, and she picked George "Bud" Gollum, a handsome twenty-year-old pre-med student and World War II veteran. Although Beulah Louise was deeply in love with her new beau, her parents were less than enthusiastic about the new relationship. In fact, they informed their daughter that if she ever married Gollum, they would refuse to give their permission. Nevertheless, Beulah Louise and Gollum did get engaged and set their nuptials for April 30, 1947.

Initial reports of the explosion on board the *Mary E.* pointed to an accident, which occasionally occurred with boats of this type because of faulty gas engines. But after a swift examination of the wreckage, police investigators discovered that the actual cause of the explosion had been dynamite and not a malfunctioning engine. Thirty-one sticks of unexploded dynamite and several detonators were found in the wrecked hull, and it was hypothesized that if the bomb had worked as it had been intended, there would likely have been no remaining evidence to raise suspicions. The first blast, investigators theorized, was supposed to trigger a second, much larger explosion that would have completely destroyed the boat and any remaining evidence. A heavy wooden wall thwarted the plan, confining the detonation and blast only to the engine room.

When the Orange County coroner examined the bodies, he discovered Walter Overell had been impaled by a wooden plank and had suffered traumatic head injuries, while his wife died of multiple skull fractures. Upon closer examination, it was determined that the couple had possibly died earlier of these injuries. A ball-peen hammer found at the scene fit neatly into the head wounds of both victims. A search of Bud Gollum's car turned up pieces of wire and adhesive tape similar to that used to prepare the bomb on the *Mary E.* There were also bloody clothes and a large assortment of sleeping pills. A sales receipt showed the young couple had purchased fifty sticks of dynamite at a store in Chatsworth on the day before the blast, with Gollum using an alias for the purchase. When questioned by police, Gollum stated that Walter Overell had asked him to pick up the explosives but denied any knowledge of what he planned to do with them. Police theorized that Walter and Beulah Overell were first beaten to death, and then the boat was blown up. They also speculated that motives for the murders included financial gain and the Overell's disapproval of Beulah's relationship with Gollum. Beulah was expected to inherit a large fortune after her parents' deaths.

The trial of Beulah Overell and Bud Gollum at the Orange County Court House, (Overell and Gollum seated second and third from the left). *Courtesy of the Los Angeles Public Library: Herald Examiner Collection.*

Four days later, Beulah Overell and Bud Gollum were arrested and charged with first-degree murder. The resulting trial attracted nationwide attention and became what was at the time described as "the trial of the century." It certainly contained all the necessary elements of intrigue: sex, wealth, lust, and greed.

While in custody, Beulah remained dispassionate and unemotional, often playing solitaire for hours on end. The two defendants also wrote love letters to each other, which were eventually leaked to the press. This only added to the melodrama and national obsession with the trial. In one of these letters Gollum wrote, "Because I love and adore and worship and cherish you with all my heart, I'll kidnap you and carry you off somewhere where no one will ever be able to find us and I'll make passionate and violent love to you. If you ever marry another person, I will kill him." Beulah Louise replied, "Would you still marry me if I were broke? Oh Pops, darling, please promise you will marry me. You're an uplifted human being. You're the most intelligent person I ever heard of. Einstein was a moron compared to you . . . Yes, sir, you're the object of my adoration and the creature of my determination."

When their dual trial began on May 26, 1947, Judge Kenneth Morrison allowed radio broadcasts of the proceedings with one restriction, the order permitted only local radio stations, and there was only one at the time: KVOE in Santa Ana. The station contracted with the Mutual Broadcasting System

Gravesite of Walter and Beulah Overell at Forest Lawn Memorial Park, Glendale.

to rebroadcast the trial throughout the country, and soon everyone was riveted to the sensational accounts.

One of the most dramatic and extraordinary murder trials in Orange County history, the proceedings lasted four-and-a-half months, which at the time was the longest such trial in American history. Defense attorney Otto Jacobs tore apart the prosecution's case, arguing that it was built entirely on circumstantial evidence; hundreds of witnesses testified.

On October 5, 1947, after two days of contentious deliberations, the jury of six women and six men agreed on a verdict of not guilty. Before the decision was read, Judge Morrison admonished spectators to remain calm and silent. Despite this warning, when the court clerk read the verdicts pandemonium ensued within the courtroom. The defendants, who had shown very little emotion throughout the entire proceedings, exhibited very little reaction as the verdict was read.

In the end, the jury determined there was sufficient evidence to determine that the Overells' deaths were not murder but suicide. Walter Overell had been suffering from severe depression and dwindling finances, which pushed him to kill himself and his wife by deliberately setting the explosion on the *Mary E.*

Now freed from custody, Beulah and Gollum were greeted on the steps of the Orange County Courthouse by hundreds of cheering spectators, who lined the front lawn to get a glimpse of the infamous duo. Gollum emerged first, flanked by his mother and sister. Beulah emerged a few minutes later with her attorneys, a large grin on her face. Asked to comment, she remarked: "Oh my! What do you think I am going to say?" Pressed about her intention to marry Gollum, she snorted with a laugh: "No!" Gollum, much calmer then his codefendant when asked about plans to marry Beulah, said softly, "We'll see."

After the trial, Gollum, who had been a student at Los Angeles City College, spent several months traveling and eventually found work with a traveling carnival. He ended up serving a year in prison in Georgia on federal charges of transporting a stolen car across state lines. He later returned to school, earned a doctorate degree in biophysics, and taught school. He moved to Northern California and then disappeared into obscurity.

A year after the trial, Beulah discovered that the huge fortune she expected to inherit from her parents was nothing close to her original estimates. She quickly dumped Gollum, married twice, and eventually moved to Las Vegas.

As the years passed, she began to drink heavily and suffered numerous health ailments. On August 24, 1965, she was found dead at her Las Vegas home. Her naked body, strewn across a bed, was found by her husband at the couple's home. Nearby stood several empty vodka bottles and a loaded .22 caliber rifle. Although her body was covered in bruises, an autopsy determined the cause of death to be acute alcoholism. She was thirty-six years old.

A Desire to Kill
LOUISE GOMES
(1947, Sacramento County)

The traditional rule for juveniles who commit crimes is that they will be tried in the juvenile court system. However, in certain circumstances, almost every state allows for youths below the age of eighteen to be tried as adults, but the rules vary from state to state.

In California, anyone fourteen years and older can be tried as an adult for serious crimes. Examples of serious crimes include murder, robbery with a weapon, and rape. But each crime case has highly individualized conditions. Each criminal is different. Each situation is different. We should not judge based on arbitrary age but by the culpability and intent of the individual offender, no matter their age, especially once they have entered puberty. The law in every state in this nation already does this, and this is why prosecutors exercise significant discretion in how they charge each offense and offender.

We don't really need studies to tell us that teenagers generally act differently; that they are sometimes impulsive, or don't fully appreciate the risks they take. They can be emotionally volatile and are often susceptible to peer pressure or stress. But this can be said for many adults as well.

The relevant issue in considering premeditated crimes committed by teens is whether or not they had the ability to know what they were doing was wrong. Criminality and culpability is defined in law and in mental health as the ability to form intent.

On the afternoon of July 21, 1947, fourteen-year-old Louise Gomes bludgeoned to death her nine-year-old foster sister, Mary Lou Roman, at their home in Elk Grove, California, a quiet agricultural community south of Sacramento. The two sisters had just finished some chores when Gomes was suddenly overwhelmed with a desire to kill. The teenager was considered very bright and had never exhibited any violent tendencies prior to the attack.

Louise was born on March 9, 1933, in San Francisco and was abandoned by her birth mother. She was adopted by Joseph Gomes and his wife three months later. In the coming years, the Gomes's supplemented Joseph's meager income at the Stockton State Mental Hospital by taking in foster children.

On the morning of the tragedy, Gomes's parents had left Louise in charge of her younger siblings so they could run some errands. As Mary Lou and Louise sat outside on the back porch, Louise suddenly erupted in a fit of rage and started choking her little sister. Mary Lou fell to the ground, and Louise picked up a club and began striking the defenseless girl until she was rendered unconscious. Not convinced Mary Lou was dead, Gomes retrieved a sledgehammer from a nearby shed and proceeded to smash the girl's head until she was certain the deed was done. Then in a calm and calculated manner, she went inside, where she cleaned up, changed clothes, and waited to see what would happen next.

A short time later, Wilda Eagan, a neighbor, stopped by the Gomes's home with some oranges to sell and found Mary Lou's body on the porch. The horrifyingly bloody scene shocked her, and she quickly left the house and sought help at another neighbor's home. Law enforcement officers were notified and arrived at the Gomes's home, where they found Mary Lou deceased, laying in a pool of blood, with Louise sitting calmly looking out the window of the living room. When confronted, Louise immediately confessed that she had killed her sister, and in a cold and unapologetic manner told stunned officers that she had harbored a secret desire to murder for more than a year. She also stated that she had attempted to satisfy this yearning by killing several small animals. She said she had initially wanted to kill her mother but settled on her younger sister because it was convenient and easier.

Louise Gomes was taken into custody and charged with first-degree murder. She pleaded not guilty by reason of insanity. Deputy District Attorney Albert H. Mundt stated that the first-degree murder charge was intended to be severe because he wanted to protect the public and keep Gomes in prison for life. Under California law, no person under the age of eighteen could be executed.

On July 26, Judge Peter J. Shields presided over a brief hearing of whether or not to try Gomes as an adult in Superior Court. During the proceedings, Rudolph Toller, a psychiatrist and superintendent of the Stockton State Hospital, testified that Gomes was "extremely dangerous . . . she would be a menace if left at large." Judge Shields ruled, "I believe she (Gomes) cannot be adequately dealt with by the Juvenile Court. It is in the best interest of society that she be tried in the Superior Court." During this brief hearing, Gomes sat calmly and appeared to be unaffected as her grief-stricken parents sat nearby. After these proceedings were concluded and just prior to being taken away by a jail matron, Louise, who had previously refused to speak with her parents, turned and casually asked her mother, "Mama, will you bring me my marbles and jacks? I have plenty of time to play now."

Although Gomes was to be tried in adult court, she was held at the county juvenile detention facility while awaiting trial. While in custody, she was blunt with officers and doctors, "Now I feel relieved it's all over. I have accomplished my desire." When asked if she felt any sadness or remorse about the killing, she chillingly stated, "I'm not sorry when anyone dies. I only cry when I get a whipping."

On September 22, Louise's defense attorneys abruptly withdrew her plea of not guilty and entered a plea of guilty to second-degree murder. Her sanity and sentencing hearing was deferred until October 14 to allow both parties time to prepare arguments. During the one-day hearing, psychiatrist Theo K. Miller testified that Gomes was in deed sane at the time of the murder but in his opinion exhibited a mental deficiency that made her "a very dangerous person not fit to be at large. One who should be confined in an institution for a very long time." The court agreed with Dr. Miller's assessment and declared Gomes to be a psychopathic delinquent and insane. She was ordered committed to the Pacific Colony at Spadra, a state mental facility near Pomona.

As the sentence was pronounced, Gomes showed no emotion and sat stoned-faced as her fate was declared. Her incarceration at the facility lasted only ninety days. On January 10, 1948, she was deemed not suitable for commitment as a psychopathic delinquent and diagnosed as a sexual psychopath who should be incarcerated at a more appropriate facility. Judge Van Dyke remanded her to the custody of the California Youth Authority, who then transferred her to the California Institute for Women in Corona.

What happened to Gomes in the following years is not known. After an exhaustive search of public records and other sources, no further information was uncovered regarding Gomes's life behind bars or whether she was ever released from custody.

Pushing up Daisies
ADA ROBERTS PETERS
(1948, Tuolumne County)

On August 18, 1948, Ada Roberts Peters, forty-one, was formally charged with first-degree murder after confessing to police that she had poisoned her boyfriend, dismembered his body, and buried it in several shallow graves at an auto campground in Sonora, California. The body of her boyfriend, Otto Hansen, forty-eight, had been found two days earlier by an employee of the campground, where the couple had been staying since December.

Peters and her companion had suffered severe financial setbacks in the recent year, and both were out of work. They had been spending the winter at the Sonora campground as a way to limit expenses. Their small savings, originally intended to be used to open a bar in Alaska, had been gradually gambled away by Hansen at the campground.

In late March, Peters casually informed neighboring campers and campground management that Hansen had left to search for work and that she had decided to stay at the campground. On July 15, Peters abruptly moved out of the campground, telling managers that she had been offered and accepted a job as a housekeeper at the Cliff House Lodge in Groveland, a short drive from Sonora.

One month later, on August 16, campers staying near the site where Peters and Hansen had been residing complained to camp managers that a rotten stench was emanating from a freshly planted flower bed near their campsite. Police were notified, and after digging around in the area, they discovered decomposed human remains buried in two shallow graves. One contained a head, legs, and arms while the second, a few feet away, contained a torso. The next day Peters was traced to a Modesto beauty salon and arrested. Also detained was Harold Weille, forty-two, with whom Peters had met while living in Sonora.

Initially, Peters told police investigators several different versions of what had happened. The first scenario had Hansen leaving for Alaska; a second account stated that his body was found dumped at the cabin; and a third and final version had Peters buying Hansen some poison so he could kill himself. She stated, "I didn't know what he wanted it for or why he took it. If I didn't do what he said, he got mean and shook me."

Finally, Peters confessed that on March 27 she gave him the poison, and he died in his sleep. For several days after the alleged suicide, Hansen's body remained in the cabin, and Peters recalled not knowing what to do. Eventually, she devised a plan in which she used a knife and hatchet to cut up his body. She then buried the body parts in two shallow graves near the cabin and covered them with flowers to mask any odors emanating from the decomposing remains. Detectives did not believe her wild story of suicide, and she was charged with first-degree murder to which she pleaded not guilty and not guilty by reason of insanity.

Her trial began on October 11. Prosecutors, who did not seek the death penalty, described the defendant as a cold-blooded murderess, who had filled a medicine capsule with poison and had given it to her unsuspecting boyfriend. It was learned that Peters, the mother of six children, had met Hansen in Lancaster, where he was employed as a bartender. It was also learned that she was twice widowed, having been married to Tom Egan, who died in a hunting accident in 1929, and Robert Peters, who had died in 1932.

Peters took the witness stand in her own defense on October 18 and testified that she had bought the strychnine at the victim's direction but denied administering it. She stated that Hansen had been in declining health for several months and had refused to see a doctor. Peters went on to state that Hansen insisted she help him kill himself and that initially she refused to assist, but under the fear of physical violence she eventually relented. Under cross examination, she had a very difficult time explaining why she had dismembered Hansen's body and buried it secretly rather than reporting the suicide to authorities. To this question, she simply stated that Hansen did not want a funeral or anyone to know what had happened.

On October 20, the jury of six men and six women began deliberating, and after only four hours of discussion found Peters guilty of first-degree murder and recommended a sentence of life in prison. Peters showed no emotion as the jury foreman read the verdict, although courtroom observers did comment that she appeared to be somewhat relieved that the ordeal was finally over. Two days later she was formally sentenced to life in prison by Judge J. T. B. Warne and ordered committed to the Tehachapi State Prison for Women. Speaking directly to the judge prior to the sentencing, she stated, "I am not a murderer, but as long as the jury has found me guilty, I will accept my sentence."

In an ironic twist of fate, Peters was the second poison-murderess convicted in Tuolumne County in nineteen years by Judge Warne, who also presided over the Eva Brandon Rablen case in 1929.

Sex, Money, and Murder in Hancock Park

BETTY FERRERI

(1948, Los Angeles)

Sensational celebrity murders and the books and films that recreate the tragic events have always been some of Hollywood's most popular exports. Readers and moviegoers delight in the lurid tales of unhappiness and darkness that often combine components of sex, greed, good-looking characters, fabulously wealthy locations, and intricate storylines. In 1948, Angelinos were held spellbound by the ghastly, sex-drenched events that emerged in one of the city's wealthiest neighborhoods. Los Angeles's Hancock Park, an affluent and historic district, has been a tree-lined sanctuary for the rich and famous since the 1920s. On October 26, 1948, the city's attention was focused on a palatial mansion on South Lucerne Boulevard, where Elizabeth "Betty" Ferreri used a meat cleaver to kill her philandering husband, who somehow survived two gunshots fired by the mansion's unbalanced caretaker.

In 1941, Elizabeth Patricia Laday, an attractive eighteen-year-old college student met Jerome Ferreri at a diner owned by her parents in New Brunswick,

Home of Jerome and Betty Ferreri, where on the night of October 26, 1948, he was shot and hacked to death by his wife. (South Lucerne Blvd., Los Angeles)

New Jersey. Ferreri, a good-looking and charismatic twenty-five-year-old, was a well-known petty criminal. His father, Vincent, was well connected within New York City politics and had suspected connections with the city's criminal underworld.

Betty was infatuated with Jerome's bravado, and their sexual attraction and chemistry was mutual. She soon began ditching school to meet up with her new suitor. Although she was well aware of his sordid past, Betty believed that with her help he would change his wicked ways. Betty's parents, who disapproved of the relationship, thought otherwise, and she was sent to live with relatives in Asbury Park, New Jersey. Undeterred, Jerome followed, and they soon eloped.

In 1943, hoping to begin a new life, Jerome and a very pregnant Betty moved to Los Angeles. Because her deadbeat husband could not hold a job and was chronically unemployed, she was forced to find work as a carhop at a local drive-in to support the family financially. In an attempt to help the struggling couple, Jerome's parents gave them the down payment on a sprawling mansion in wealthy Hancock Park, and to supplement their meager bank account, they began renting rooms to boarders. They also hired fifty-two-year-old Alan Adron as the estate's caretaker.

Jerome Ferreri cherished the good life, and although his wife's meager paychecks could not afford such a luxurious lifestyle, somehow he always had enough cash on hand, thanks to his parents. Always in need of attention, Jerome would often cruise the streets of Los Angeles looking for women while his wife toiled away at work. During their short marriage, the only thing Betty Ferreri could count on were regular beatings from her husband that gradually increased in severity.

During the early morning hours of October 26, 1948, Jerome Ferreri arrived home with another young woman. Enraged by his brazen and callous behavior, Betty threatened the pair, and they were forced to flee the house. Realizing that her husband would at some point return home, and fearing for her life, Betty asked caretaker Alan Adron for protection. When Jerome did return home several hours later, he angrily confronted his wife, and a violent physical altercation ensued in which Betty was dragged by the hair into the butler's pantry. Hearing her screams, Charles Fauci, a thirty-five-year-old boarder at the house, gave Adron a revolver. In a scene of utter chaos, the feebleminded caretaker rushed to Betty's aid and without saying a word shot Jerome Ferreri twice. Although he was mortally wounded, Jerome was not dead. Fearing he might renew his attack, Betty grabbed a meat cleaver from the counter of the pantry and began viciously hacking her husband until she was certain he was deceased.

A few minutes later, police arrived at the scene and arrested Betty, Fauci, and Adron. All three defendants were charged with first-degree murder, and local news media quickly dubbed her the "Cleaver Widow." Over the next several months, the public, egged on by an overzealous news media, was captivated by the salacious accounts of the murder and adulterous activities of the victim. Prosecutors admitted that Jerome Ferreri was a horrible husband, but Betty and her alleged accomplices had planned and premeditated his murder. Jack Hardy, who initially represented all three of the defendants, responded that his client had endured years of emotional and physical abuse at the hands of a philandering husband, and the toll of these abuses had finally pushed her over the top.

During the trial, which began on February 8, 1949, the defense's version of the events featured an abused woman's self-defense claim that included indisputable evidence of the victim's violent behavior and numerous infidelities, while prosecutors portrayed Betty as a cold and calculating killer, who had premeditated the murder of her husband with the help of her accomplices.

Deputy district attorney J. Miller Levy admitted that the victim had been "tempestuous, obstreperous, ferocious, turbulent, quarrelsome, and vicious." But he also argued that Betty had willingly engaged in sexual relations with her husband and that the murder had been premeditated.

Defense attorney Jack Hardy countered that Betty was a vulnerable woman, duped by her playboy husband. She was a victim, Hardy argued, of years of verbal torment and physical abuse who finally just snapped.

Alan Adron refused to allow Hardy to portray him as crazy, and he hired his own attorney, Gladys Towles. She argued that he was temporarily insane at the time of the shooting; but in a twist, alleged that he had been under a hypnotic trance at the time but was now clear-headed. Because of these allegations, the news media mockingly dubbed him "Robot Man."

On the first day of trial, Adron shocked the courtroom by pleading guilty to the charges and agreed to testify for the prosecution. In so doing, Adron stated that the shooting was planned in advance but only an hour before the actual slaying. Betty Ferreri's defense attorneys quickly minimized the damage by presenting Adron's unstable mental health history as evidence of his feeblemindedness and unreliability as a witness.

Throughout the proceedings, the defense mounted a continuous and calculated assault on the victim's character, insinuating that his years of philandering and brutal treatment of his wife ultimately contributed to his own demise. At times during the emotional testimony, Betty was unable to control her reactions and had to be shielded from spectators in the courtroom.

When she eventually testified in her own defense, Betty shocked the courtroom with tearful allegations of relentless abuse suffered at the hands of her husband throughout their marriage. She describe her deceased husband as a "sadist, an incorrigible brute, a bully, a beast" who nonetheless looked at her with "big puppy-dog eyes." According to Betty, "sometimes he gagged me and locked me in a bedroom closet, threatening to kill me and my unborn baby if I made a sound, forcing me to endure the sounds of his lovemaking to another woman. When he let me out, he expected me to cook for him."

Stories of Jerome's philandering were endless. Unable to control her emotions while discussing her relationship with her husband, on her last day of testimony she collapsed on the witness stand, producing one of the trial's many dramatic interruptions.

On March 18, the prosecution and defense summed up their cases, and the jury of five women and seven men began deliberations. The following day, after several hours of heated debate and two ballots, jurors acquitted Betty Ferreri and Charles Fauci. After the verdict was read, exuberant friends and relatives rushed to Betty's side as she sat stunned while her codefendant sat nearby practically unnoticed. The jury foreman later explained the verdict to the press, stating that they had believed the defendant's sincerity and seen her actions in the terms of "hysterical" self-defense. They also found that Jerome Ferreri's abusive character was an overriding factor in their conclusion; he had clearly deserved what he got, and the prosecution had failed to prove their case with any reliable evidence.

Eleven days later, on March 29, Alan Adron was found not guilty by reason of insanity by Judge Fricke. During the brief hearing, psychiatrists testified that he suffered from recurring bouts of dementia and was not a dangerous man. At the time of the slaying, his actions were blamed on his living environment—namely the tension and bedlam of the Ferreri home. On April 8, a lunacy commission hearing found Adron to be mentally ill and ordered him hospitalized. Several months later he was deemed sane enough to be released from custody.

A few months after her acquittal, Betty found herself back in court, this time fighting five traffic tickets she had collected since her release. "The Wilshire police are persecuting me," she said. "And all you have to do is drive a Cadillac around here to get a ticket." She eventually paid a small fine to avoid jail time. On August 21, she married twenty-eight-year-old Jean-Paul Roussos, a maître di' at a ritzy Hollywood nightclub. The couple was wed at the Wee Kirk o' the Heather Chapel in Las Vegas. Whether the couple lived happily ever after is not known because no further information was discovered after 1950.

Conclusion

"There are crimes of passion
and crimes of logic. The
boundary between them is not
clearly defined."

—Albert Camus (1913–1960)
French philosopher, author, and journalist

The forty-six women discussed in the pages of this book committed their crimes for a variety of reasons. Women like Laura Fair, Lastenia Abarta, and Marie Leonard Bailey killed because their men lied about marriage plans and violated their reputations in the process of their respective affairs, while others claimed insanity, as did Katie Cook, Beatrice Mallette, Betty Hardaker, and Betty Ferreri. These women were depicted as victims, but over time, defense of such crimes shifted due to advances in psychiatry and changes in the law. Defense attorneys depicted their clients as victims, while prosecutors claimed the acts were against morality and law. Women such as Clara Wellman had been beaten and abused by a husband who also terrorized the community in which they lived; he thus deserved to die. Angela Maria De Vita killed to protect her family. Lea Delmon slew the man who tried to sell her into prostitution. Betty Ferreri killed because her man needed to be killed. Many of these women believed the only power they possessed was the power to destroy their tormentor.

Other female criminals were identified with greed as the root of their murderous acts. The cases of Aurelia Scheck, Gertrude Gibbons, Louise Peete, Madalynne Obenchain, Rosa Tarlazzi, and Beulah Overell contained elements of this motive for their crimes. Defense attorneys often depicted these female defendants as victims of a materialistic society who overly valued income and status. For some, such as Louise Peete and Juanita Spinelli, their relations with men—other than killing them—did not reflect middle-class values, and there was no credible excuse as to why they had committed murder.

Whether 1850 or 1950, the cases of women accused of murder or other crimes demonstrated that gender mattered. Female stereotypes such as appearance and demeanor were constructed for the male-dominated courtroom and system. The press was also instrumental in controlling the outcomes of these cases by revealing (true and false) facts of the crimes, while also narrowly focusing on the performance of witnesses and lawyers, rarely mentioning the law. They also helped amplify and contribute to the negative stereotypes associated with female criminals of the time period.

The ultimate purpose of this book was not to glorify criminals or the crimes they committed. Rather, it was deliberately written to be an unbiased description of facts. From this it is hoped the reader has found a better understanding of the psychology and senselessness of these acts. Some of these crimes were more sensational than others, some were more baffling, and some were more audacious, while almost all were shocking and appalling. The notorious female crimes revisited in this book were all of these things and much more, but the end of this book is not the conclusion of the story. In the second half of the twentieth century and beyond, California would play host to an overabundance of infamous female criminals.

To be continued ...

Afterword

by Jill Leslie Rosenbaum,
Ph.D.
Professor of Criminal
Justice

While interest in criminal behavior began in the mid-eighteenth century, the first scientific studies took place in the late nineteenth century. During the time frame 1850–1950, when the crimes Michael Thomas Barry describes here were committed, the field of criminology was developing at a rapid rate. Yet, there was little attention paid to crimes committed by women. While criminologists developed numerous theories to explain criminality in the late nineteenth and early twentieth centuries, those explanations were limited to the behavior of men. The rationale for excluding women from any serious study of crime was the fact that women committed fewer crimes than men, and those they did commit were generally less serious and often sexual in nature.

WHY WOMEN COMMIT CRIMES
(1895–1960)

Indicative of the lack of interest in female crime, of all the books written about criminal behavior, only three pertained to women. The first, *The Female Offender* (Lombroso and Ferrero, 1895), argued that women were biologically primitive and less evolved than men, had more "evil tendencies" than men, any "maternal instincts" and "ladylike" qualities were suppressed and, thus, less sensitive to pain, less compassionate, jealous, and full of revenge. The second, *The Unadjusted Girl* (Thomas, 1923) portrayed female offenders as thrill seekers, who were unable to control their sexual appetites. Finally, Otto Pollack in *The Criminality of Women* (1950) argued that crime data do not adequately reflect the amount of female crime because their crimes are less likely to be reported, and even when they are, they receive preferential treatment by the criminal justice system. Although these studies were seriously flawed, you see their influence in how the offenders discussed in this book are perceived and treated by both the community and the criminal justice system.

WHY WOMEN COMMIT CRIMES
(1975-Present)

Between the latter parts of the nineteenth century up until the mid-1970s, while female offenders were being touted as evil and unable to control their sexual impulses and their offending was seen as a result of individual pathology, criminologists were attributing social factors (class, status, culture, family problems, bad companions, etc.) to male criminality. However, the women's movement gained momentum and the crime rate among women (though still quite small) began to rise, Adler (1975) and Simon (1975) argued that the emancipation of women was related to their increased involvement in crime. In other words, as women entered the world of work, their behavior would become more like men. It is important to note that while the women's movement had the greatest influence and opened more doors for white, educated women, women who find their way into the criminal justice system are primarily poor, women of color, with less education. Thus, while little evidence existed to back up their claims, their work led the way to more thorough, systematic studies of female offenders.

Until the 1990s, criminology was, for the most part, "constructed by men" to "explain men." However, the last twenty-five years has seen the emergence of feminist criminology. These theories build upon the themes of gender roles and socialization. Rather than see the female offender as "sick," there is an attempt to look at background in order to understand who she is, where she came from, and why she engages in crime. To date, one of the most important findings is that there are specific pathways that lead women into crime. For instance, one pathway is the result of the woman's prior victimization; incarcerated women have a much higher rate of physical, emotional, and sexual abuse than female non-offenders (Belknap and Holsinger, 1998). Other pathways include younger, single mothers who suffer from depression, women who live in high crime areas with high rates of poverty and lacking adequate vocational skills, or women who are antisocial and aggressive and are unable to develop a stable environment. Understanding the pathways women take into offending allows us to understand how women become stuck in a cycle that often leads to offending. As a result of feminist research, we now have a greater understanding of what motivates women to commit crimes and how they differ from their male counterparts. The life circumstances that are specific to women including childbirth, child care, care of the sick and elderly, abuse by men, dependence upon men—play an important role in their pathways to criminality.

RECENT ARREST DATA FOR WOMEN

According to recent data collected by the FBI (Uniform Crime Report, 2016), women represent approximately 25% of all of those arrested in the United States. In sheer numbers, 287,487 men and 73,754 women were arrested in the United States for violent crimes in 2015. With regards to homicide arrests nationwide, 6,639 men and 880 women were arrested during the same year. In California 1,439 people were arrested for murder, 89.2% (1,284) men and 10.8% (155) women. These figures are consistent with an analysis of United States arrest data from 1980 to 2008, which indicated that women accounted for 10% of homicide arrests, 20% of arrests for violent crimes, and 37% of arrests for property crimes nationally (US Department of Justice, 2010). While there has been an increase in the arrest, conviction, and incarceration of women, much of this rise is the result of both the growth in drug use and abuse and changes in policy, enforcement, and mandatory sentencing, in particular, the war on drugs.

WHAT WE KNOW ABOUT WOMEN WHO MURDER

One of the most consistent findings is that regardless of how you measure crime, women commit fewer crimes than men. Thus, women who are charged with homicide are less likely to have a criminal record. While men are more likely to murder a stranger, women's victims are more likely to be intimate partners or family members. Their offenses take place in private, in self-defense, and are motivated by fear. Furthermore, they are more likely to commit the offense alone and are more likely to be victims of domestic violence (van Wormer and Roberts, 2009). It is important to note that 75% of victims murdered by an intimate partner are women. This figure has remained relatively constant for the last three decades. However, prior to the appearance of victim protection services, domestic violence shelters, and other services afforded these victims, males and females murdered their partners at the same rate. When women are given a means of escape from dangerous situations, they are more likely to take advantage of them. As van Wormer and Roberts (2009) argue, this occurs because men's and women's motives for murdering their partners are different; men are likely to murder a partner for retaliation after a breakup or attempt to leave, while women act out of self-defense. Thus, women are often still at risk even after they leave the relationship.

ARE FEMALE OFFENDERS TREATED DIFFERENTLY THAN MALE OFFENDERS?

It is commonly believed that the criminal justice system treats female offenders more leniently than males. An examination of the US Sentencing Commission records indicated the sentences of white women with similar crimes and criminal history were 9.5 months shorter than males (Sarnnikar, Sorenson, and Oaxaca, 2007). Other research indicates that women who are masculine in appearance or who do not show gender appropriate demeanor are treated more harshly than more feminine appearing women (Belknap, 2007). Furthermore, there is evidence that indicates both prosecutors and the media tend to emphasize the masculine characteristics or lesbianism of female offenders and portray them as "man-hating" women who are the personification of evil (Baker, 2012; Farr, 2004). In addition, research indicates that younger women, poor women, women of color, immigrants, and lesbians are not granted the leniency that is granted white women who appear to be feminine in their demeanor (Bloom, Owen, and Covington, 2004).

Discrepancy in sentencing may be most apparent in death penalty sentences. While women make up approximately 11% of those serving time for murder in America, they make up only 1.4% of those on death row. In fact, only fifteen women have been executed since the death penalty was reinstated in 1976 (Carson, 2015). While on the surface it appears that courts are reluctant to sentence women to death and, perhaps, too chivalrous to carry out the execution, that is not the case. The reason women are less likely to be sentenced to death has to do with the fact that women commit different kinds of murder than men. As previously mentioned, women who murder most often kill an intimate partner. Proof of premeditation is a necessary requirement to be convicted of a capital murder, thus the types of murder women most often commit do not meet this condition. In addition, most men have much longer and more serious criminal histories, which also affects the sentencing of offenders.

UNDERSTANDING FEMALE OFFENDERS: THEN AND NOW

If we look at the forty-six women portrayed in this book, it is clear that little difference exists between women who killed then and women who kill now. As is true today, the women Barry has identified murdered someone who was known to them and, in most cases, a spouse or family member. Also true today, the majority of the women you have read about were victims of emotional, physical, or sexual abuse. Women such as Hattie Woolstein, Isabella Andross. Bridget Waters, Clara Wellman, Lea Delman, Nettie Platz, and Edna Mallette were all victims of domestic violence and would be good candidates for the defense known today as the Battered Women's Defense. Others, including Josephine Valenti, Mary Anna Cox, and Betty Hardaker, murdered their children or someone who was under their care, which is also the second largest group of victims of female murderers today. Effie Scholl and Edna May Fuller's pathway to criminality included poor living conditions, financial struggles, and various mental health issues. And, then, as now, the "Black Widow" or "Gold-Digger" (e.g., Louise Peete, Mary Hartman, Eva Braden Rablen) are often the cases that receive the greatest amount of attention because they fit the stereotype of the evil woman.

Woven through popular culture today is the bad girl, the evil woman, the deranged female stalker. Cable television hosts an entire show, *Snapped*, that focuses solely on actual cases of women who commit murder. Movies (*Fatal Attraction, Chicago*, etc.) depict both true and fictional examples of women who stalk, torture, and murder their victims. In addition, television broadcasts of gavel-to-gavel coverage of notable cases (i.e. Pamela Smart, Casey Anthony, Jodi Arias) feed the public's hunger for gory details. These cases have become the basis for many Lifetime television movies and the plot for many other crime-related TV shows. The growing number of examples found throughout popular culture indicates the extent of the allure. Whether 1850 or 2018, gender does influence how offenders are dealt with in the criminal justice system, portrayed in the media, and perceived by the public.

AFTERWORD REFERENCES

Adler, Freda. 1975. *Sisters in Crime: The Rise of the New Female Criminal*. New York: New Press.

Baker, D. V. 2012. "A Contextual History of Black Women's Executions" in R. Muraskin, *Women and Justice: It's a Crime*. Boston: Prentice Hall.

Belknap, J. and Holsinger, K. 1998. "An Overview of Delinquent Girls: How Theory and Practice Have Failed" in R. Zaplin, *Female Crime and Delinquency*. Gathersberg, MD: Aspen Publishing.

Belknap, Joanne. 2007. *The Invisible Women*. Belmont, CA: Thomas Wadsworth.

Bloom, B., Owen, B., and Covington, S. 2004. "Women Offenders and the Gendered Effects of Public Policy." *Review of Policy Research*. 21(1) 31-48.

Carson, Ann. 2015. Prisoners in 2014. NCJ248955. Washington DC: Bureau of Justice Statistics.

Lombroso, C. and Ferrero, G. 1895. *The Female Offender*. New York: D. Appleton and Co.

Pollack, O. 1950. *The Criminality of Women*. Philadelphia: University of Pennsylvania Press.

Sarnikar, S., Sorenson, T. and Oaxaca, R. 2007. "Do you Receive a lighter prison sentence because you are a woman?" IZA Discussion Paper No. 2870. http://ssrn.com/abstract=999358.

Simon, Rita. 1975. *Women in Crime*. Lexington, MA: Lexington Books.

Thomas, W. I. 1923. *The Unadjusted Girl*. Boston: Little Brown and Co.

UCR 2016. *Crime in the United States*. Federal Bureau of Investigation. Washington, D.C.

BIBLIOGRAPHY

Amador Ledger. Jackson, CA: Various Years and Dates.

Anzilotti, Cara. *She-Devil in the City of Angels*. Santa Barbara, CA: Praeger
   Publishing, 2016.

Bakken, Gordon, and Brenda Farrington. *Women Who Kill Men*. Lincoln, NB:
   University of Nebraska Press, 2009.

Cairns, Kathleen. *The Enigma Woman: The Death Sentence of Nellie May
   Madison*. Lincoln, NB: Bison Books, 2009.

Caughey, John Walton. *California*. Upper Saddle River, NJ: Prentice-Hall, 1940.

Church, Madeline. *Emma LeDoux and the Trunk Murder*. Luxemberg Publications,
   1995.

Cullum, George. *Biographical Register of the Officers and Graduates of the U.S.
   Military Academy*. Vol. 1. New York, NY: Van Nostrand, 1868.

Daily Alta California. San Francisco, CA: Various Years and Dates.

Duke, Thomas S. *Celebrated Criminal Cases of America*. San Francisco, CA:
   James H. Barry, 1910.

Fresno Bee. Fresno, CA: Various Years and Dates.

Haber, Carole. *The Trials of Laura Fair: Sex, Murder, and Insanity in the Victorian
   West*. Chapel Hill, NC: The University of North Carolina Press, 2013.

Hynd, Alan. *The Case of the Attic Lover and Other True Crime Stories*. New York,
   NY: Pyramid Books, 1958.

Ireland, Robert. "Frenzied and Fallen Females: Woman and Sexual Dishonor in
   the 19th Century United States." *Journal of Woman's History 3*. NY: Binghamp-
   ton University, Vestal (Winter 1992).

Jones, Richard Glyn. *The Mammoth Book of Women Who Kill*. New York, NY:
   Carroll & Graf, 2002.

Kipling, Rudyard. *Rudyard Kipling's Verse: Inclusive Edition, 1885–1918*.
   London: Hodder & Stoughton, 1919.

Los Angeles Herald. Los Angeles, CA: Various Years and Dates.

Los Angeles Times. Los Angeles, CA: Various Years and Dates.

Manly, William. *Death Valley in '49*. Los Angeles, CA: Borden Publishing Co., 1949.

Mann, William J. *Tinseltown: Murder, Morphine, and Madness at the Dawn of Hollywood*. New York, NY: Harper-Collins Paperbacks, 2014.

Newton, Michael. *The Encyclopedia of Serial Killers*. Los Angeles, CA: Checkmark Books, 2006. First published 1999 by Facts on File.

Oakland Tribune. Oakland, CA: Various Years and Dates.

Odell, Robin. *The Mammoth Book of Bizarre Crimes*. New York, NY: Hachette Book Group, 2010.

Offord, Lenore. *The Gifts of Cordelia: The Case of Cordelia Botkin*. NY: Dual, Sloan & Pierce, 1947.

Rice, Richard. *The Elusive Eden: A New History of California*. New York, NY: McGraw Hill, 1996.

Riverside Daily Press. Riverside, CA: Various Years and Dates.

Robbins, Millie. *Tales of Love and Hate in Old San Francisco*. San Francisco, CA: Chronicle Books, 1971.

Royce, Josiah. *California: A Study of American Character: From the Conquest in 1846 to the Second Vigilance Committee in San Francisco*. Berkeley, CA: California Legacy Books, 2002.

Sacramento Daily Union. Sacramento, CA: Various Years and Dates.

San Bernardino Sun. San Bernardino, CA: Various Years and Dates.

San Francisco Call. San Francisco, CA: Various Years and Dates.

San Francisco Chronicle. San Francisco, CA: Various Years and Dates.

Santa Ana Register. Santa Ana, CA: Various Years and Dates.

Santa Cruz Sentinel. Santa Cruz, CA: Various Years and Dates.

Segrave, Kerry. *Lynchings of Women in the United States: The Recorded Cases, 1851–1946*. Jefferson: Jefferson, NC: McFarland & Company, Inc., Publishers, 2010.

Smith, Erica L. and Alexia Cooper. *Patterns & Trends—Homicide in the U.S. Known to Law Enforcement, 2011.* United States Department of Justice: Bureau of Justice Statistics, December 2013, www.bjs.gov/content/pub/pdf/hus11.pdf.

Taylor, Quintard. *In Search of the Racial Frontier.* New York, NY: W. W. Norton & Company, 1998.

Van Nuys News. Van Nuys, CA: Various Years and Dates.

Vronsky, Peter. *Female Serial Killers: How and Why Women Become Monsters.* New York, NY: Berkley Books, 2007.

INDEX

A –

Abarta, Hortensia 28
Abarta, Lastenia 27–30, 157
Abarta, Pierre "Pedro" 27
Adron, Alan 154–156
Ambrose, Thomas 124
Andross, Isabella 35–38
Anselmo, Carrie 40
Appel, Joe 73–74

B –

Bailey, Edwin 71
Bailey, Marie Leonard 71–72, 157
Ballard, Wesley 49
Barbey, Emeline 30, 32
Barton, Jim 49–51
Beale, Silvia 60–62
Beale, William 60–62
Beard, James S. 61–62
Bevo, Abele 62–63
Blescar, Ruth 107–108
Bosley, Henry 73
Botkin, Cordelia 15, 44–48
Bradley, Belle 117
Brown, William 117
Bryan, William Jennings 144
Burch, Arthur 80–85
Burdick, Nellie Clarice 114–116

C –

Cabrillo, Juan Rodriguez 35
Caffee, Peggy 90–94
Cannon, Fred 21–23
Capone, Al 135
Carlson, Esther 110–112
Casey, James 87
Cash, Leland S. 135
Cazaux, Augustin 30
Cheney, William 33–34, 37
Chipp, Dora 60–62
Coleman, Harry A. 121

Cook, Carroll 46
Cook, Katie 48–51, 53, 157
Cook, Thomas J. 48–51
Coughlin, Raymond T. 136
Cox, Beatrice May 126–127
Cox, Charles Kenneth 138
Cox, Clara 126–127
Cox, Mary Anna 138–139, 163
Cox, Winnifred May 138–139
Crittenden, Alexander Parker 23–26
Crum, Arthur 123

D –

Darcy, Patrick 32
Darrow, Clarence 144
Davis, Barton 132–133
Davis, Chloe 131–134
Davis, Le Comte 50
Davis, Lolita 131
Deane, Ida 45
Delmon, Lea 63–64, 157, 163
Delmon, Louis 63–64
Denton, Jacob Charles 74–75
De Vita, Angela 62–63, 157
Duffy, Clinton 78, 137
Dunning, John Preston 44–48
Dunning, Mary Elizabeth 44

E –

Eagan, Wilda 149
Erickson, Anna 110–112

F –

Fair, Laura 23–26, 54, 157
Fauci, Charles 154–156
Faurote, Harry 74
Ferreri, Betty 15, 153–157
Ferreri, Jerome 153–156
Fitts, Buron 95
Forster, Francisco "Chico" 27–30
Forster, John "Don Juan" 27, 30
Fricke, Charles 117, 156
Fuller, Edna May 96–97, 164
Fuller, Otto 96–97

G –

Gates, Walter S. 96

Gibbons, Frank 67–69

Gibbons, Gertrude 67–69

Godfrey, John F. 29

Gollum, George "Bud" 144–148

Gomes, Joseph 149

Gomes, Louise 148–150

Gomes, Mary Lou 149

Griggsby, John 48, 49

Gunness, Belle 111–112

H –

Hamilton, Frank 53

Hamilton, Joseph 54

Hammond, Anna 65–66

Hammond, Charles 65–66

Hansen, Otto 151–152

Hardaker, Betty 128–131, 157, 163

Hardaker, Charles 129–131

Hardaker, Geraldine 128–131

Hardy, Jack 155

Harlan, Charles 31–35

Hartman, Henry 98–99

Hartman, Mary 98–99, 164

Hartman, Oluff 98–99

Hartman, Ruth 98–99

Hawkins, Gordon 135–138

Head, Mary 57

Healy, Joe 56

Hedrick, Ray 90

Heinrich, Edward O. 101

Herrick, Josiah 68

Hogan, Clarence 71–72

Hogan, John T. 35

Hollis, Lillian 26

I –

Ives, Albert 135–138

J –

Jackson, Andrew 23

Judson, Lee Borden 76–78

K –

Karnes, Etta 129
Karnes, Samuel 129
Kavanaugh, Edward 104–105
Kavanaugh, Marcy 104–105
Kelly, Edward 127
Kennedy, J. Belton 81–85
Klumb, Roy 87

L –

Lafarge, Marie 98
Landreth, Harold B. 78
Larsen, Albert 53
Lassere, Faustin 65–66
Latham, Emily 76
LeDoux, Emma 15, 54–58
LeDoux, Eugene 55
Lee, Anna (see Louise Peete) 76
Levy, J. Miller 155
Lindstrom, August 110–112
Lindstrom, Peter H. 111
Liszt, Franz 140
Logan, Arthur 76–78
Logan, Margaret 76–78

M –

Madison, Eric 117–119
Madison, Nellie May 116–119
Mallette, Edna Beatrice 122–124, 157, 163
Mallette, Louis 122–124
Mansfeldt, Annie Irene 139–143
Mansfeldt, Hugo 140
Mansfeldt, John 140–143
Marcy, Jessie 76
Marsh, James 98
Marshall, Charles 53
Martin, Patrick 39
Martin, Vada 140–143
Maurer, Charles 97
May, Hazel 120
May, John 120
McVicar, Albert Newton 55–58
Meadows, Alberta Tremaine 90–94
Merriam, Frank 90–94

Miller, Joe 55–58
Miller, Theo K. 150
Montgomery, Victor 50
Moody, Mabel 49–50
Morrison, Kenneth 146–147
Mundt, Albert H. 149
Murphy, Edward 142–143
Murrillo, Custodia Vasquez 109–110
Murrillo, Rosa 109–110

N -

Neidman, Henry 35–38
Nutter, William A. 57

O -

Obenchain, Madalynne 80–85, 157
Oesterreich, Fred 86–90
Oesterreich, Walburga "Dolly" 86–90
Olson, Culbert 137
Overell, Beulah 144–148, 157
Overell, Walter 144–145

P -

Peete, Louise (see Anna Lee) 15, 73–78, 157, 164
Peete, Richard 74
Penington, John Brown 44
Penmark, Rhoda 131–134
Peters, Ada Roberts 151–152
Phillips, Armour 90–94
Phillips, Clara 90–94
Phillips, Elizabeth 50
Pico, Pio 27
Platts, Inez 95
Platz, Earnest 79
Platz, Nettie 79, 163
Pons, Louise 64
Preston, John 45

Q -

Quayle, William 83

R -

Rablen, Carroll 100–102
Rablen, Eva Brandon 100–102, 152, 164

Rada, Ysabel 27
Rawson, Delia 51
Rector, Edward N. 121
Rolph, James 102, 105
Roman, Mary Lou 148
Rossi, Mario 114–116
Roussos, Jean–Paul 156

S –

Sanhuber, Otto 87–90
Scheck, Aurelia 58–60, 157
Scheck, Joel 58–60
Scholl, Effie 41–44, 164
Scholl, Orr 41–42
Scopes, John 144
Segovia, Josefa 20–23
Sepulveda, Ygnacio 29
Shapiro, Herman 87–89
Sherrod, Robert 135–138
Shields, Peter J. 149
Shinn, Horace 33
Simone, Michael 134–138
Spinelli, Juanita 15, 134–138, 157
Stackpole, Ernest Gary 58–60
Steele, Nettie 95

T –

Talkington, Bertha 119–121
Talkington, Esther 120
Talkington, Lamar 119–121
Tarlazzi, Dorothy 107–109
Tarlazzi, Frank 107–109
Tarlazzi, Rosa 107–109, 157
Thompson, Alsa 94–96
Thompson, Claire 94
Thompson, Maxine 94
Thompson, Russell 95
Towles, Gladys 155
Twain, Mark 26

V –

Valenti, Josephine 102–104, 163
Valenti, Sabatini 102–104

Warne, James 101, 152
Waters, Bridget 38–41, 163
Waters, Peter 39–41
Weille, Harold 151
Wellman, Clara 53–54, 157, 163
Wellman, Frank Pingrey 53–54
Wells, Guilford Wiley 29, 33
White, Stephen M. 33
Williams, William 55
Willis, Frank R. 76
Wood, Fred V. 115
Woolsteen, Hattie 30–35, 163
Woolsteen, Minnie 31
Woolwine, Thomas 83

Yutang, Lin 78

Michael Thomas Barry is the award winning author of seven nonfiction books that include *Murder and Mayhem: 52 Crimes that Shocked Early California 1849-1949* and *In the Company of Evil —Thirty Years of California Crime, 1950-1980*. Among his many literary awards are the 2011 and 2014 Readers' Favorite International Book Awards (silver and gold medals) and 2017 Independent Publisher Book Award (bronze medal). Michael is also a columnist for CrimeMagazine.com, where he pens the column "This Week in Crime History." He resides with his wife, Christyn, and their golden retriever, Jake, in Orange, California.